12-2006
SCHLEICHER CO.
BOX 611-201 S. MAIN
ELDORADO, T
D0042298
DATE DUE

MAD AS HELL

ALSO BY

MIKE

LUPICA

NONFICTION

REGGIE
(with Reggie Jackson)

PARCELLS:
THE BIGGEST GIANT OF THEM ALL
(with Bill Parcells)

WAIT TILL NEXT YEAR
(with William Goldman)

SHOOTING FROM THE LIP

FICTION

DEAD AIR

EXTRA CREDITS

LIMITED PARTNER

JUMP

How Sports Got Away from the Fans—and How We Get It Back

Mike Lupica

G. P. PUTNAM'S SONS
NEW YORK

G. P. Putnam's Sons
Publishers Since 1838
200 Madison Avenue
New York, NY 10016

Published simultaneously in Canada

Library of Congress Cataloging-in-Publication Data

Lupica, Mike.
Mad as hell: how sports got away from the fans—and how we
get it back / by Mike Lupica
p. cm.
ISBN 0-399-14221-5 (alk. paper)
1. Professional sports—United States. 2. Sports—Corrupt
practices—United States. 3. Sports spectators—United
States—Attitudes. I. Title.
GV583.L698 1996 96-26409 CIP
796'.0973—dc20

Printed in the United States of America

10 9 8 7 6 5 4 3 2 1

This book is printed on acid-free paper. ♾

Book design by Brian Mulligan

ACKNOWLEDGMENTS

This book would not have been possible without the friendship, support, and legwork I got from Jeremy Schaap. He has already won a Sports Emmy for writing he did for the *Outside the Lines* series on ESPN, and has worked as both a print reporter and on television. Jeremy is just twenty-six. Wherever he finally ends up, in newspapers or magazines or working as an on-air reporter, he is going to be a big star.

I just hope his next employer can fit him under the salary cap.

As it turns out, I have had the great fortune over the last several years to sit next to Jeremy's father, Dick, every Sunday on *The Sports Reporters*. Dick Schaap has done just about everything you can do in this business, from newspaper columns to the thirty books he has written to his current jobs reporting for ABC News and ESPN. I have always considered him to be a champion in all phases of this game, and an inspiration to me. When it was time to start *Mad as Hell*, his son seemed like a perfect choice to ride shotgun. And he was just that: a perfect choice. Occasionally, I felt like his assistant. His talent and passion are all over these pages.

And of course there would never have been a book without two people: First, the great Esther Newberg of International Creative Management, who had been telling me for a couple of years to go start writing every time I would start complaining again about what I was seeing in sports. And second, a gentleman, in all ways, named Neil Nyren. I knew before I started that he was one of the best editors in the business. What I didn't know was his capacity for friendship. He sat in his office at Putnam about a week before Christmas 1995 and listened to my rant about sports, and when I was through, he said, "Let's do it." Only, I could never have done it without his input, his encouragement, his sense of what to put in and what to leave out, and his ability—for several hectic months, anyway—to operate with both skill and calm while feeling as if he were putting out a daily newspaper. He shaped this book from the start. He is one of those guys we are always looking for in sports, the ones who make you lift your game.

Thanks also go to Susan Kirk of Business Resources, New Canaan, Connecticut, who took the edited pages Neil kept sending me every few weeks, and assembled all the pieces of the puzzle with skill, on the fly. She was another one who kept her head when the whole thing started to feel like a fire drill. She is a pro. So is Sean Carr of ABC News, whose research and fact-checking were so invaluable to me.

I must thank friends who listened so well, so patiently, and helped out so much. Jimmy Breslin, one of my writing heroes, once said that the real trick in life is hanging around with people smarter than you. Which I do with Pete Hamill and William Goldman on every writing project of my life. Joe Valerio, my producer at *The Sports Reporters* and an ex-sportswriter who helped give me my start in newspapers back in 1975, made himself available for counseling sessions when I needed them. So did Barry Stanton, the fine

Gannett sports columnist, and Michael Solomon of *Esquire*, and, as always, Dick Berkowitz, world's greatest barrister.

Finally, I want to thank my father and mother, who made me believe from the start that sports could give me a wonderful life. Just because they know every possible thing there is to know about wonderful lives.

—Mike Lupica
New Canaan, Connecticut
June 1996

This book is for my wife, Taylor, and
for my three sons, Christopher, Alex, and Zach.
I say here what I say all the time:
I love them to the sky and back.

Contents

MAD AS HELL

INTRODUCTION

Sports owners have always been scum.

Players have always been greedy.

The average fan has always been treated like crap.

But I'm getting ahead of myself.

There is more sports available to the American fan, sitting in the stands or just grazing in front of the television, than at any other time in the history of the known universe. And there are more fans available to sports. The most recent Super Bowl, Super Bowl XXX, drew a television audience of a mere 138 million people, and the first three days of the Summer Olympics in Atlanta, 139 million people watched on NBC. Every time you think sports can't possibly grow any more, it does, sort of like Marlon Brando.

It is not just that there are more teams and games and televised games. You now have networks devoted solely to covering sports and reporting the sports news. You have channels devoted to individual sports such as golf. Something called the Classic Sports Network showed up on certain cable systems in 1996, just so no one had to miss anything from the days before every touchdown and touchdown dance and crotch grab was shown on ESPN's *SportsCenter.* If you felt as if you got cheated because television didn't cover sports in the fifties the way it does now, there was now a spot on the dial for you. You could watch Willie Mays make that over-the-shoulder catch off Vic Wertz all day long.

It isn't just television. The background noise you now hear in sports, all day long, from coast to coast, is the constant howl of all-sports radio. You have that for company when you are driving home from the ballpark or going to the ballpark or just on your way to the 7-Eleven between games for more corn chips.

If there really is such a thing as between games in this country anymore.

When you shut off the television and turn off the radio, you can fire up your laptop and go on-line now and have statistics and results available with almost bewildering speed, speed that makes some sports fans almost moist with excitement. There's a reason why so many fans think of sports as sex, just much safer. One morning, I listened to a couple of sports talk hosts in New York conduct a poll of their male listeners:

Would they rather have sex on Sunday afternoon or watch the football games?

Football ran away the way Secretariat did that time at the Belmont Stakes.

So if you want to, you can go on-line and find out about a basket in Sacramento or Vancouver before the other team has pushed the ball back over halfcourt. This, of course, is for the squirrely fans who can't wait for the latest score to scroll past on television, or wait for the next sports update on all-sports radio.

Waiting for the morning paper to get scores is considered something for sissies. The modern sports fan, armed with all this information, light-headed to have this kind of access, is better informed than any policy wonk in Washington. Once it seemed as if Cable America would provide more than enough sports for even the worst sports nerds. Only, cable wasn't enough. So now there is something called DIRECTV, a small satellite dish you can hook up on the side of your house that replaces those big ugly things you tried to hide in the backyard, but couldn't, because they looked like the spaceship Tom Hanks brought home in *Apollo 13*. You buy DIRECTV, and then, for an extra fee, you can order up most of the National Basketball Association season. Or the National Hockey League season. Or the whole baseball season. I can sit in my den in Connecticut and switch back and forth on a Sunday night between Shaquille O'Neal playing the Utah Jazz in the Great Western Forum and Michael Jordan going against the Nuggets in Denver. I tell myself that this is all about my job.

But I'm like everybody else: The access makes me pretty hot. Why? Because that little dish has become sports' newest sex toy.

At least for the time being.

If I wanted to pay more—and had no wife or children or life—I could order up every college basketball game, every night of the winter, from Maine to New Mexico.

Sports has been as big a twentieth-century entertainment phenomenon as the movies or television or anything that has happened or will happen with computers. Baseball was invented more than 100 years ago, but other than Ken Burns, who really cares? Sports was not even a significant part of American life until the 1920s, and did not explode until the second half of the century. Now it is a dominant part of our culture, and our lives, and especially our language. It is a national obsession without any boundaries for age; in that way, it is much more an obsession than rock-and-roll music. Not everybody knows Mick Jagger. You better believe that everybody knows Michael Jordan.

There isn't a political race anywhere that is not described with the language of sports, and its metaphors, until the experts just absolutely wear your ass out, sitting around on panel shows and sounding like a bunch of drunken sportswriters in the bar, trying to out-cliché each other.

In so many ways, this should be the Golden Age of American sports, as we approach the next century, hunkered down and bunkered down with our software and our dishes and our remote-control switchers and all our other toys. There was supposed to have been one other Golden Age, back in the twenties, because of Babe Ruth and Jack Dempsey. It never happened, the way Damon Runyon's *Guys and Dolls* New York never happened. As the writer Jimmy Breslin pointed out in his 1991 book about Runyon, Runyon simply invented his own version of Broadway, a Big Street where the gangsters all had hearts of gold and so did the bimbos on their arms. Somehow the whole thing became an accepted part of American history anyway. Sportswriters made up the so-called Golden Age of sports the same way, just without Runyon's magic with words and characters. There were no television highlights to police anybody. So everyone was a hero and everything was bigger than life.

The sportswriters didn't make everything up, of course, the way they made up Dempsey. Ruth did hit all those home runs and Yankee Stadium really was The House That Ruth Built. The rest of it was fiction, and potboiler fiction at that. Bill Tilden was the great American tennis star of the 1920s, a major star of the so-called Golden Age, and it wasn't until after Tilden was dead and buried that anybody pointed out that Tilden was as interested in ballboys as he was in collecting Grand Slam titles.

These should be glory days, and real ones, for the American sports fan. More games. More teams. More cool merchandise to wear. Video games for the kids to play. Cable and satellites and the worldwide web. As much action as you could ever want. More action than Vegas, without leaving your den. If you've gone all the way over the edge, you can even carry a little beeperlike device with you wherever you go, one that runs scores the way Headline News runs them at the bottom of the screen.

Only this isn't a Golden Age of sports at all, no matter how much we watch and buy and listen and care. At a time when modern fans are bombarded with more of everything and armed with more of everything, like spoiled kids, here is where they really are at the end of the day:

More pissed off than they have ever been.

If there is one prevailing emotion with most fans, it is this:

The whole thing has gotten away from us.

And how do we get it back?

And as angry as fans are, they feel powerless at the same time. They are mad as hell, and occasionally do yell out the window—right next to the DIRECTV dish on the side of the house—that they aren't going to take it anymore. But then they lie down until the feeling passes. They know they are going to keep taking it from sports, because there is no place to go. There is no sports congressman to whom they can write. There is no Supreme Court or Justice Department of sports. There is no law, because if there is one thing that is absolutely crystal clear to the modern fan, it is that the bastards who run everything just keep making up the law as they go along. We all saw what happened when Bill Clinton tried to end the baseball strike of 1994 and 1995: The players and owners treated him with about the same respect they treated some fat slob spilling beer all over the row in front of him in the left-field bleachers.

So the fan sits by and has nothing to say when ticket prices go up. Again. The fan sees more and more teams and bigger and bigger salaries, and then takes a close look at the teams and the players making the money, and what he really sees is this relentless mediocrity. The fan settles for the mediocrity. So he (or she, don't wear me out with this) sees good presented to him as great, by sportswriters and broadcasters who either can't tell the difference anymore or don't care to. And before anybody knows it, great has turned into immortal.

That is how a couple of posturing, preening self-promoters like Andre Agassi and Deion Sanders became legendary American sports figures before they'd ever won anything. They were talented enough, had enough of an act, and—most important—gave good sneaker commercial.

The fan does what he always does:

He sits back and watches it happen.

Watches the worst set of caretakers in baseball's history—the current crop of owners—do everything to what was once this country's national pastime except throw gasoline and set it on fire. There is another strike, they cancel the World Series in 1994, and all across the country you hear this from fans:

That's it, these people have gone too far this time, I've had enough, I'm never going back to the ballpark.

But they always go back.

Why?

Because they need their games, that's why.

More and more, the modern fan feels like someone trapped in an abusive relationship, with everybody involved in big-time sports: commissioners and owners and players and agents, the network guys pimping for them. In one way or another, the fan gets abused by all of them. In ticket prices. In cable prices. The price of a goddamn hot dog at the ballpark. The fans nod while being told that they have to pay more because the players are making more.

And after all of that, you know what happens? One of two things:

1. The owner threatens to move their team, to Los Angeles or St. Louis or Baltimore or Nashville, if he doesn't get a new ballpark or a better ballpark;
2. The owner *does* move the team.

It's supposed to be the Golden Age of sports, and it's become the age when ballparks are more important in sports than the people sitting in them. Because those are the big sex toys, for the big boys of sports. If we won't give them one, or finance one, they will find someone who will, don't worry about that.

They have already gone through our pockets. They have already gotten at least some of their financing from our tax dollars. All the while telling us they are on our side, that everything they are doing is good for us. Then, if we are lucky, they give us the courtesy of waving good-bye from the window of the moving vans.

Because no matter how badly they have screwed up our teams, and ultimately screwed us, there is always another city ready to reward them.

Art Modell is the has-been who spent about thirty years trying to slowly run the Cleveland Browns into Lake Erie. Modell, who saw sellout after sellout in Cleveland Stadium, 60,000 and 70,000 fans every Sunday from the sixties on, eventually put together the kind of debt that would make even a member of the Royal Family blush. By the summer of 1995, he had managed—he said—to put himself about $60 million in the hole. He said he'd blown it all on the Browns. No one believed him.

By then, people in Cleveland wouldn't have believed Art Modell if he told them Lake Erie was wet.

And you don't need cable television or the worldwide web or a beeper or DIRECTV to figure out what happened next.

Modell won the lottery!

It was as if those two guys from Publishers Clearing House showed up on his doorstep and announced he won the ten million bucks. Only in Modell's case, it was hundreds of millions from the city of Baltimore. The guys handing over the money were the mayor of Baltimore and the governor of Maryland.

And in the case of Georgia Frontiere—the ex-showgirl who ended up with the Rams when Carroll Rosenbloom, her sixth or seventh husband, drowned in the Atlantic Ocean—it was the mayor of St. Louis and governor of Missouri who came courting. Frontiere didn't offer to marry either one of them. She had something much sexier than an aging showgirl to offer them:

The Rams.

Baltimore had once been screwed out of the Colts, and St. Louis had been screwed out of the Cardinals. They screamed their moral outrage and righteous indignation about the injustice of it all to the high heavens. Then, the very first chance they got, they showed the world that they like this kind of screwing in sports much better when they get to be on top.

Of course, all of this is even older than Georgia Frontiere. You want to know who the first real free agent was in sports? A fat, ham-faced, cigar-smoking Irishman from Brooklyn named Walter O'Malley, who moved the Dodgers to Los Angeles in 1957.

Other teams had moved before the Dodgers left Brooklyn. The Braves had left Boston for Milwaukee, and the St. Louis Browns had moved to Baltimore—Baltimore does have a certain skill at grabbing teams known as the Browns—but no one had ever made the kind of score O'Malley did. He had a baseball team, and Los Angeles wanted to be in the big leagues and basically handed over acres of prime real estate in downtown L.A. to him. And that was the start. There had been other rich and powerful owners in baseball before O'Malley. But no one ever saw the future in sports the way he did, the possibilities. O'Malley was the first to figure out the game of city against city. All modern sports hustlers are disciples of him. He is their patron saint.

You know where Art Modell grew up, by the way? Brooklyn, New York. He probably cried himself to sleep when O'Malley took his beloved Bums. But in the end, Modell and everybody else in Brooklyn who had been supporting the Dodgers in Ebbets Field didn't matter to O'Malley any more than Browns fans mattered to Modell.

We don't matter to any of them.

They tell us we do.

We don't.

They know that if we get out of the ticket line, someone else will take our place. That is why the First Commandment of modern sports is this one:

Go ahead and love your team. Just don't expect it to love you back.

And they don't just want our money. They want our loyalty, too, and they want it right now.

"They" can mean owners or players; it's too much of a pain in the ass to tell them apart anymore.

Once, there was a huge distinction in sports between management and labor. No more. They all have the same sense of entitlement, even if they say they don't. The players do thank God once in a while after the game. They just never thank *us*.

The players just move on to the next team and the team moves on to the next city. It used to be that if you screwed up a team in sports, you had to sell it. Now the owners just start packing, because the next city has set things up for them like it's Club Med.

The owners, of course, blame their free agency on the players' free agency. If you listen to modern sports owners long enough, sports owners will blame everything except Bosnia on free agency. They've been saying it from the time when free agency entered sports for good in the middle of the 1970s, and they will always be saying it, and it will always sound like more crap from them.

Just not as much as I once thought.

Both owners and players have fought over free agency, and stopped seasons because of free agency, and used it whenever they could to make a few more dollars. Baseball players waited the first seventy-five years of the century to have the same basic rights that

I've sure had as a newspaperman, and people in most other jobs have had: the ability to move, at the end of a contract, from one place to another. And when free agency did come to baseball in the middle of the 1970s, it was greeted by the liberals and civil libertarians among us as the most noble and necessary idea since the Emancipation Proclamation. Jesus, just talking about it made us feel virtuous.

Marvin Miller, the former executive director of the Major League Baseball Players Association, became one of the most powerful and successful union leaders in this century. Curt Flood is the ballplayer who first put himself on the line, challenging the legality of baseball's reserve clause, which basically bound a player to a club for the life of his career. Flood finally lost his case in the Supreme Court, but then two pitchers—Andy Messersmith and Dave McNally—finally won against baseball, and were declared free agents. And the genie was out of the bottle.

The whole thing, though, was Marvin Miller's baby from the start, the way the modern sports union is his baby, the model for all the other unions in all the other sports. Miller fought the baseball law, and the law eventually got its ass kicked.

Sports was never going to be the same, for any of us.

Free agency turned out to be a success for Miller's ballplayers, and eventually ballplayers in the other sports, beyond any dreams Curt Flood or Messersmith or McNally could possibly have had way back at the beginning.

At the end of the day, though, it has been a disaster for the fan. In the words of an old country-and-western song, they got the gold and we got the shaft.

Free agency—not all the time, but most of the time—has ruined the one thing that burned sports into our hearts and imagination and memory in the first place: It stole our relationship with the players, and with our teams. And it stole our history. Because we don't know these people anymore. We recognize the uniforms, if they haven't changed those as part of some big marketing scheme. We recognize the caps, if they haven't changed those. But way too many of the players are strangers. No one grows up with a team the way Brooklyn grew up with the Boys of Summer in the fifties, the way Yankee fans grew up with Yankee teams of the same era who were in the World Series all but two times between 1948 and 1965. Mickey Mantle was there for all but one season of that glorious Yankee run, as was Yogi Berra, as was Whitey Ford. Of course, in those days the players stayed only because they had no choice. And the owners even screwed Mantle on money every chance they could. And the crowds weren't as big then as they are now. The whole business of sports wasn't as big.

Just better.

Things didn't change about every twenty minutes. That doesn't mean sports didn't need change, couldn't be changed for the better. Flood will never be remembered the way Jackie Robinson is, but his courage altered the business of sports the way Robinson altered, forever, the look of sports.

But here is something that cannot be changed in sports: Players constantly moving from city to city and owners now doing the same thing—you really can't talk about one without talking about the other—has been a terrific deal for them and a lousy deal for the fans, except in the short run.

Only, sports wasn't ever supposed to be about the short run.

The romance of sports, from the beginning, was that it was going to be forever. Now rooting for your players in professional sports, wherever that team is, is like rooting for players in college. You know you're only going to have the players for a certain amount of time, two years or three or four.

That's if the college players don't leave school early, using their own form of free agency.

There is no question that free agency was an idea whose time had come.

So were afternoon talk shows.

Over the years, all the way back to the first professional baseball in the nineteenth century, professional sports in this country was slowly built up into the most legitimate plantation society left in American life. Free agency made Players vs. Owners into a fair fight at last.

We as fans just didn't know at the time that both sides were going to turn around when they got tired of fighting with each other, and beat the living daylights out of us.

The war between owners and players goes on to this day and will always go on, in some form or fashion. And we're always going to be the ones expected to do most of the financing, all the way up to these luxury boxes that have become the high-class whorehouses of American sports. There is no argument or debate about sports being bigger than ever. Sports is bigger, and the country is bigger, and money in the country is bigger. More people with more to spend, and a ton of that money, every single day, gets spent on sports. The numbers are there in a way they have never been before, no matter how fondly we look back on the past.

But if you think bigger always means better in sports, you should be sentenced to a lifetime of watching one 1–0 game after another in World Cup soccer.

(By the way, when the World Cup came to the United States, all the soccer nerds in this country had the same mantra for all of us who couldn't bother watching the 1–0 games: Two billion people around the world can't be wrong about soccer. Meaning all the countries besides this one where soccer is king. My answer was, This kind of mistake has been made before. Just look at how many people have watched *Cats.*)

All you have to do these days is listen.

If there is one crucial service that sports-talk radio provides, it is this: It is an ongoing record, at full pitch, of all the anger out there. Everybody involved in sports ought to listen to the amount of bitching that goes on. The guys who host sports radio shows in this country want to believe they are the whole truth about sports and nothing but the truth. They want us all to believe that the opinions shouted back and forth on these shows—to the point where you can't tell the callers from the hosts half the time—are some kind of Gallup poll on a particular issue. They're not.

But if you listen long enough, what you hear more than any opinion about this player or that one, this manager or that coach, is the constant, twenty-four-hour-a-day, anger.

What these people are really doing is shouting across the great divide between Us and Them.

You want to know why Magic Johnson's brief comeback touched everybody the way it did (at least at the beginning, before he began to act like another Generation X brat and had to retire all over again)? Because there was that brief time when he reminded us that there were still some pro athletes, and big ones, who seemed to care about the games as deeply as we do. This wasn't another asshole doing a dance because he had managed to tackle somebody. Or dunk the ball. ("My father told me something when I was a kid, and I never forgot it," Grant Hill told me one time. "When you dunk the ball, act as if you've done that before." It is one of the reasons why Hill gets more All-Star votes than anybody these days. Grace still matters.) This wasn't somebody grabbing his crotch because he caught a touchdown pass or hit the ball over the fence, confusing excitement with arousal.

Magic Johnson in those first months back was still someone whose love for the game, always strong but now made stronger by absence, shone through every time he came up the court with the ball. He loved being out there as much as we loved having him back. And that doesn't mean everybody has to smile the way Magic did, or have that kind of personality, that kind of love for applause and spotlight and cheers. No one has ever accused Grant Hill or Cal Ripken, Jr., of being the life of the party. But Hill's love for the game, his respect for the game, shines through. So does Ripken's, every day, ever game, every year.

They don't act as if they're doing time.

Or doing us a favor.

During the NBA's All-Star Weekend in February of 1996, Shaquille O'Neal was discussing his impending free agency and said, "I'm a businessman."

This is an example of Shaq sounding as if his nickname should be Schmuck.

As in: "No you're not, Schmuck. You're an athlete and an entertainer. Now, go bust another backboard."

When Michael Jordan came back to basketball after his fling with baseball, he went on and on about his love for the game, to the point where he began to sound preachy. Or as if this was some new marketing campaign for him, to sell Nike shoes and Gatorade and Jockey shorts. Jordan is the greatest basketball player who ever lived, but not everything he says is gospel, let's face it. Remember, he said he was retiring from the Bulls a few years ago because he wanted to spend more time with his family, and immediately ran off to join the baseball circus.

Even the biggest guys can snow us sometimes; it's just a question of how much they think they can get away with. Even the biggest stars, like Jordan, can sometimes seem about as sincere as a starlet.

But Jordan had obviously been looking around and listening while he was down there in the bush leagues with a lot of time on his hands between strikeouts, and he was smart enough to figure out something.

Fans were good and pissed off. Why? In basketball, they were tired of seeing the young stars Jordan had left behind making jerks of themselves every time they turned around. It wasn't the epidemic some people tried to make it out to be. There were still as many Grant Hills coming into the game as there were punks like Derrick Coleman. But too much of it, way too much of it, was going around. One of the summers Jordan was away, the American basketball team called Dream Team II—following in the footsteps of the Jordan–Johnson–Larry Bird Dream Team the United States had sent to the Barcelona Olympics—went to basketball's World Championships in Canada and tried to turn the whole thing into a crotch-grabbing festival.

"We're just expressing ourselves," Reggie Miller said afterward.

The basic reaction to Miller's comment went like this: We're all for artistic expression, kid. Just keep your hand out of your pants, okay?

I like Miller, but he just sounded like another modern athlete who didn't get it. The way baseball players who showed up for union meetings in limousines during their strike didn't get it. The way the Dallas Cowboys during the week before Super Bowl XXX didn't understand why people had a problem with them showing up for practice in white stretch limousines.

"What difference does it make to fans how we get there?" asked Nate Newton, one of the Cowboys with the biggest mouths.

Jesus, these people have gotten dumb about sports.

Mostly about fans.

Fans still matter in sports. They're tired of being told they don't.

It's time for them to do something about it, or forever hold their peace.

Chapter One

A CONFEDERACY OF DUNCES

Chapter one, verse one, in the Bible for all sports fans:

Owners don't know anything more about sports than we do.

Most of the time, they know a hell of a lot less.

They are a lot like our elected officials in that way, except in one crucial way: When elected officials turn out to be the kind of screwups we get in sports on a regular basis, at least there is the opportunity for us to vote them out of office on Election Day the way we voted them in.

But there is never Election Day in sports, as much as we need one. There is Opening Day and Banner Day and all the rest of it. Just never a day when we get to talk and they have to listen.

They've got their team, and unless one of them gets completely out of hand—the way an old catcher's mitt like Marge Schott finally did—we are usually stuck with them for life.

For what feels like a life sentence.

It's not just sports, by the way. All you have to do is look around. Other big shots make a mess out of big companies all the time. If you don't think so, take a look at what a sparkling job Laurence Tisch did with CBS. Even though Tisch has a brother named Robert who owns half the New York Giants, it is Laurence who acts dumb enough to be a sports owner. Because Laurence Tisch didn't just have one team, he really had half the National Football League. CBS had owned rights to the league's NFC conference games since the NFL-AFL merger, and before there was an AFL, CBS had pro football to itself in the 1950s and '60s, and really invented pro football coverage in this country. Pro football was identified with the network as much as any program it had ever aired, from *I Love Lucy* to *60 Minutes*. For four decades of Sunday afternoons, you had football on CBS. By the 1970s, because of the huge boom in pro football, those games provided a fabulous lead-in for *60 Minutes* on Sunday nights, another reason why *60 Minutes* seemed as if it had been a Top 10 show forever.

And you know what Laurence Tisch, who was supposed to be the business genius in the family, did about all that?

He blew the franchise.

Pro football, he said, had gotten much too expensive. So when the network's contract with the NFL ran out after the 1993 season, Tisch decided he wasn't going to get into a bidding war with Rupert Murdoch's Fox network for the NFC rights. CBS president Peter Lund—think of him as the president of the team—told him CBS needed football, it was the foundation of CBS Sports, and CBS Sports had always been the foundation of the network.

Tisch said forget it.

Fox took football away from CBS. If Tisch didn't understand the value of sports—never to be confused with the price tag of sports—Rupert Murdoch sure did. Getting football moved him into the network big leagues once and for all, and, at the same time, made CBS Sports, a bedrock of the entire company all the way back to William Paley, feel like the minors. CBS lost football, it lost prestige, it lost stars like John Madden, it lost Sunday afternoons.

Laurence Tisch was just another rich, tough, smart guy acting like a complete moron as soon as he got anywhere near sports.

Happens all the time.

The people who play the games can make complete donkeys of themselves, and make us completely crazy. They can try to blow their careers because of dope and booze and sex and battering women and breaking the law. And no matter how much of this goes on, no matter how offensive and obnoxious and illegal the behavior we get from the jocks, they are never as dangerous to sports as owners. The players are at least the most talented people in the world at their jobs.

Owners are way down the food chain.

Waaaaay down.

The number-one thing wrong with sports in this country, the biggest problem, biggest and ongoing, is the owners.

They are more our enemies than any overpaid punk free agent.

Chapter one, verse two: Owners are more the enemy than anything.

The sports section was once called the toy department of newspapers, and there are still too many team owners who look at sports as the toy department of big business. There was a time in this country when someone like Colonel Jacob Ruppert, who had made his fortune as a brewer, could even look at a monster baseball dynasty like the New York Yankees as some sort of rich-boy diversion. It doesn't work that way anymore, but most of the owners—all the ones who still view their sports teams as secondary businesses—don't seem to get that.

It's just one of the things they don't get. The rest of the list is longer than *Ulysses*.

It doesn't matter who these guys are, how rich they are, how powerful they are, what kind of successes they have been in other businesses, where they stand in the Fortune 500. Ted Turner has become one of the most celebrated Americans of the last half of the twentieth century, a television visionary and pioneer, a diplomat and a humanitarian. If you don't judge him too harshly for verbal skills that sound remarkably like the late Junior Sample's, and for frequently falling asleep on wife Jane Fonda's shoulder during crucial moments in World Series games, you really have to call Turner a genius.

Not in sports.

"This ain't business!" he roared at one of his team executives one day in the 1970s. "This is fun!"

The only reason Turner's Braves finally started making the World Series in the early 1990s was that he finally got out of the way, stopped acting like some goober fan behind the dugout (he even managed the Braves for a game once—and lost, of course), and turned the operation over to real baseball people like Bobby Cox, who started out as the Braves' general manager and finally became manager, and John Schuerholz, a front-office man who had won the World Series with the Kansas City Royals and eventually did the same thing with the Braves.

And Turner's basketball team, the Hawks?

No one even knows they're in town most of the time. They've never gotten close to an NBA title, aren't likely to anytime soon. Waitresses at Hooters restaurants have a higher profile in Atlanta than Hawks players.

Point? You can invent CNN, use CNN to make the world feel like a small town sometimes, eventually become *Time* magazine's Man of the Year, marry Jane, even skipper a boat that wins the America's Cup, and still know less about the business of sports than a groundhog.

The frightening thing is, Turner isn't even remotely unusual. Even before the Braves started winning again, when both the Braves and Hawks were loser teams, Turner could come up looking like the brightest kid in class if you graded him against the curve. You must always remember that Turner is in the same business as people like this:

MARGE SCHOTT: She is the Eva Braun wanna-be who owns the Cincinnati Reds. Yes, I know she's been suspended again, but she still owns the team. She once bragged that she collects Nazi memorabilia, allegedly referred to some of her ballplayers as "million-dollar niggers," once said she didn't want her players wearing earrings because "only fruits" wear earrings. She has had a series of dogs who often distinguished themselves by mistaking home plate at Riverfront Stadium for a fire hydrant.

Maybe you're starting to get the idea.

A regular Eleanor Roosevelt.

In 1995, the Reds somehow made it back to the playoffs, led by manager Davey Johnson. Before the season had even begun, Schott had decided to replace Johnson. There was never a good reason given why. It was just another example of Marge doing to her ballclub what her dogs like to do at Riverfront.

On what was supposed to be Opening Day for the Reds in 1996, home-plate umpire John McSherry dropped dead of a massive coronary just a few moments after the first pitch. One member of McSherry's crew went into the ambulance with McSherry, the other two members of the crew stayed behind, and finally decided that the only thing to do was postpone the game until the next day.

Marge wanted to play.

"[McSherry] wouldn't want to make fifty thousand people unhappy, would he?" she said.

The guy had some nerve, dropping dead on her that way.

BRUCE MCNALL: A rich baby-faced fat boy from the 1980s. He bought Wayne Gretzky from the Edmonton Oilers at a time when it looked as if McNall was trying to buy the whole world. Thought nothing of paying a fortune for rare baseball cards. Owned the Toronto Argonauts in the Canadian Football League. Thought if he threw enough money around and sucked around enough Hollywood celebrities, he could become a celebrity himself. McNall ended up with more fraud charges against him than Gretzky had goals.

BILL BIDWILL: He owns the Arizona Cardinals, which used to be the St. Louis Cardinals. He took the Cardinals to Arizona when Arizona offered him one of those sweetheart, steal-your-team deals. Then Bidwill looked around and became sick with jealousy when he saw the kind of deal Georgia Frontiere got from St. Louis, the town he'd left for a sweetheart deal of his own. A horrible case of luxury-box envy. Then, after the ex-showgirl, oft-married, Football Widow Frontiere made her score in St. Louis, Bidwill saw all the goodies Art Modell got in Baltimore.

So before Bidwill had been in Arizona a decade, he was looking to do to Arizona what he had already done to St. Louis, and get out.

Bidwill will always chase a dollar the way Robert Packwood chased interns. While he does, he gets one losing season after another with the Cardinals. They haven't ever won anything with him owning the team, and won't ever win anything, because when you are as dumb about football as he is, you are equally dumb about football people. He has bailed out on one city and is already looking to bail out on another, but as long as he has his team, some new city will always find him adorable.

GEORGE STEINBRENNER: Over the last two decades, he has become the poster boy for the pushy, headline-hungry owners of sports. He doesn't care. Steinbrenner needs to see his name in the paper the way the rest of us need oxygen. When he first got the Yankees, he showed early speed with free agents, and used them to build World Series champions in 1977 and 1978. The Yankees have not won a World Series since. The most famous name in sports, the team that once owned October, a team that has won 33 pennants and 22 Series, has not even played in the Series since 1981 (1996 is still up for grabs as I write this). In the process, Steinbrenner has become the most hated sports figure in New York City since Walter O'Malley.

O'Malley reached that distinction by leaving. Steinbrenner is reviled, even by his own team's fans, because they are stuck with him.

He is the only owner in history every kicked out of his sport twice. The first time was for illegal campaign contributions to Richard Nixon's reelection campaign in 1972.

The second time was for paying a little bedbug of a gambler named Howie Spira $40,000 for damaging information on Dave Winfield, one of Steinbrenner's own players.

When then baseball commissioner Fay Vincent kicked Steinbrenner out the second time, the news was greeted at Yankee Stadium with a standing ovation.

LEON HESS: He has made more money in the oil business, all over the world, then a sheikh. He has also owned the New York Jets for the last thirty years. In that time, the Jets have had exactly six winning seasons. The team once played at Shea Stadium, then moved to Giants Stadium, to essentially become a tenant of the New York Giants, because Hess thought the bathrooms weren't clean enough at Shea. A couple of years ago, the old man fired Pete Carroll as his coach and hired Rich Kotite, a former Jets assistant whose Eagles team had just lost its last seven games in a row. The day he announced he was hiring Kotite, Hess growled, "I'm eighty years old and I want to win now."

The Jets promptly went 3–13 under Kotite.

"I love Leon Hess," one NFL owner told me. "And the way he runs his football team, let me tell you something: I hope he lives to be a hundred."

ROBERT TISCH: Amiable brother of Laurence. At the NFL owners' meeting in Chicago when they finally voted to allow Art Modell to move the Browns to Baltimore, Tisch came out of the vote with the same goofy smile he wears in the Giants' locker room after games, still trying to match the players' names with their uniform numbers. A reporter asked Tisch how the vote had gone.

"Twenty to five in favor of the move," he said pleasantly.

The reporter asked, "What about the other five votes?"

"What other five votes?"

"Mr. Tisch, there are thirty teams in the league."

"There are that many now?" the man who owns 50 percent of the Giants said.

TOM WERNER: There is no rule in sports that you have to be as old as Robert Tisch or Leon Hess to have your fellow owners wish you a long life.

Tom Werner, Harvard-educated, Hollywood-trained, is one of the most successful producers of situation comedies in the history of network television. His credits include *The Cosby Show* and *Roseanne,* and if that's the way you start out, it doesn't really matter where you finish.

Werner, one of those Rotisserie People, who spend half their waking hours thinking about fantasy trades for their fantasy leagues, thought it would be fun to own his very own team.

Rotisserie ball, just with real players!

(Robin Williams once said that cocaine was God's way of telling people they made too much money; Rotisserie baseball is His way of telling a lot of other people they have way too much time on their hands.)

Anyway, Werner and some of his Hollywood pals bought the San Diego Padres, just down the Pacific Coast Highway from L.A.

The Padres turned out to be funnier than Cosby and Roseanne put together. And Tom Werner turned out to be another sports dope. And as soon as he and his partners started to lose money, when old Cos couldn't wander into the scene and save them with a few jokes, everybody panicked. All of a sudden, Werner, operating in one of the biggest cities in the country, started singing the small-market blues. He started blaming The System for the Padres' inability to win and make money, even though he had a pretty good team in place, with a pretty good future, when he bought the Padres in 1990.

Werner lasted four years as a baseball owner. It just seemed longer, especially in San Diego. He was in over his head from the start, no matter how much he wanted to blame baseball for his problems. Everybody could see he was in over his head. But while he was nearly ruining the franchise, Werner was shaping the future of the sport on television. (This was the same sort of thinking that got Bud Selig his job as baseball's interim commissioner for life. In all the years he had owned the Milwaukee Brewers, the team had made it to one World Series, in 1982. Usually they field a team that would have its hands full with that women's touring team, the Silver Bullets. This is the guy the owners picked to run the whole sport. It is like taking the head of a failing UHF station and handing over ABC to him. Only in sports do the biggest screwups somehow end up with the most power.)

So Werner was one of the people who came up with a brilliant idea called The Baseball Network, which regionalized the sport not only during the regular season but during the playoffs as well. For the first time in history, baseball fans did not have access to every pitch of the postseason if they wanted it. The reason? Werner and his pals on baseball's television committee looked at baseball's dwindling ratings for the league championship series and decided that not enough fans did want to see every pitch, or every game.

So when baseball went to an extra round of the playoffs in October of 1995, there were nights when four games were being played. You got to watch one.

It was almost as neat an idea from Werner as having Roseanne sing the national anthem before a Padres game one time. She sang off-key, grabbed her crotch as if she were a Dream Team basketball player, spit at the end, and infuriated the entire country.

The Baseball Network is gone now. The San Diego Padres, under new ownership, are a contender again. Tom Werner is back in Hollywood, where the object of the game is being as funny as Werner was as an owner and baseball power broker. And where, if you lay an egg the size of Roseanne, they don't wait for you to hold your own going-out-of-business sale.

They just cancel your sorry ass.

Tom Werner didn't set out to turn his ballpark into an empty stadium, a baseball embarrassment that finally saw the upper deck covered by curtains, as if they were more aesthetically pleasing than seats without customers in them. Leon Hess would like to win another Super Bowl before he dies. In February of 1996, in the space of about three weeks, Hess laid out $17 million in bonuses to free agents and committed to an additional $44 million in salaries to be paid out over the next five years. The Jets also had the No. 1 pick in the upcoming NFL draft, and that was expected to cost Hess another $10 to $15 million. The price tag for him, just in new players between one season and the next, would end up being around $75 million. This is what you do when you are one of the world's smartest oil guys and one of the world's dumbest sports guys. Since Joe Namath walked off the field after Super Bowl III after beating the Colts, shocking the world, putting the American Football Conference on the map forever, the Jets have had those six winning seasons and won just three playoff games. They have a losing record for the 1970s, the 1980s, and the 1990s.

Hess's money hasn't done anything to stop it in the past and it probably won't do anything to help him now.

Imagine how his fans feel. But Jets fans can't fire Leon Hess and they can't force him to sell the team. They are a slave to his judgment and to his mistakes. And they keep paying and paying and paying. A Jets fan I know once said this to me, on the day he renewed his season tickets for the twenty-fifth consecutive year:

"Every year, I think about giving up my season tickets. And every year I re-up again. I stuck with these bastards at Shea Stadium, and now I schlepp over to New Jersey every Sunday. And I'll tell you why: because I live in terror that the year I give up my tickets is the year they finally start to turn things around."

One fan speaking for all the fans. People say all the time that it is money that has done the most to change sports and ruin sports in this country. The owners are the ones who say that the most. And they are the biggest problem. It's not the money, it's the moneymen.

"You grow up a fan and you dream about owning your own team, and then you finally do," one football owner told me. "You're finally a part of the inner circle. And you look around at the rest of the people in the room, the rest of the inner circle, and it just absolutely scares the shit out of you."

SO WHAT DO WE DO?

There are rules in place, in all the sports, about franchise relocation. It's just that enforcing them has become a part-time job, especially in the National Football League. But the language is there, in football and every other sport. This particular language comes from the NHL Bylaws, but really could come from anywhere:

> "36.5 . . . In determining whether to consent the transfer of a Member Club's franchise to a different city or borough pursuant to Section 4.2 of the Constitution, each Member Club shall be guided by the following considerations:
>
> > Whether the club in question is financially viable in its present location and, if not, whether there is a reasonable prospect . . . that it could become financially viable there, either under its present ownership or under new ownership.
> >
> > The extent to which fans have historically supported the club in its present location.
> >
> > The extent to which the club has historically operated profitably or at a loss in its present location.
> >
> > Whether the present owner of the club has made a good faith effort to find prospective purchasers who are prepared to continue operating the club in its present location and/or has engaged in good faith negotiations with such prospective purchasers.
> >
> > Whether there is any prospective purchaser of the

> club and franchise who is prepared to continue operating the club in its present location, and, if so, whether any such prospective purchaser is willing and able, if necessary, to sustain losses during the initial years of its operation there.

Let's make an even simpler rule.

There is no way to stop having another rich dope buy sports teams any more than the league can stop the same dope from moving the team. If the National Football League had any real backup from the courts, the Raiders would have never left Oakland or Los Angeles, the Browns would still be in Cleveland, and the Rams would have never moved to St. Louis because the Cardinals would still have been there.

And the league wouldn't have gone through an entire season without pro football in Los Angeles, the second-biggest market in the country.

But from now on, all sports leagues should enforce a more rigorous prenup than they already have on the books.

This prenuptial agreement would be signed by any prospective owner, the league, and the city in which his team is located. And the basis of the agreement would be simple enough for someone like Bidwill or Marge Schott to understand:

If I screw this team up, I will not move it, I will sell it.

Period.

Sign it, date it, have the notary stamp it.

"I am going to do everything in my power to get a new stadium built for the Patriots," Patriots owner Robert Kraft, a Bostonian, was saying in the winter of 1996. "I have been doing everything in my power. But if I can't, this team isn't going anywhere. I'll sell it."

Before buying the Patriots, Kraft had dabbled in professional sports once; if you can call the 1970s version of World Team Tennis—a team called the Boston Lobsters—professional sports.

Nearly twenty years later, with the Patriots seemingly on the verge of going to St. Louis, (this was before the Rams went after Georgia Frontiere), Kraft came along like the rich-boy cavalry to keep the Patriots at their present address, at Foxboro Stadium, about twenty minutes outside Boston. And he knew coming in that he would need a new stadium to survive with the Patriots.

Why?

Sports owners apparently need new stadiums, and new licensing agreements, and luxury boxes, the way the rest of us need oxygen. You look into the distant future—that is two or three years in sports—and you can see entire stadiums made up solely of luxury boxes, like some kind of 747 with nothing but first-class seats.

But Kraft also says this:

"I was on *This Week With David Brinkley* the morning of the Super Bowl [Super Bowl XXX, Cowboys vs. Steelers], and I think it was Sam Donaldson who compared owning a sports team to owning a dry-cleaning franchise. But I told him it wasn't. I told him something I believe, that owning a team like the Patriots, any team, is being caretaker of a public trust. And I take that very seriously. I walk through our parking lots before games sometimes, and I feel a tremendous sense of responsibility—and accountability—with these fans. This team matters to them, and mattered long before I came along. These Sunday afternoons are an important part of their life. We can't take those Sundays and just move on to the next city and not worry about the people we leave behind."

I know, I know: In the world of big-time sports, he sounds like some alien who just arrived from the Third Rock from the Sun.

I believe Kraft when he says he is willing to sell the Patriots if he can't make them financially viable. I believe he would put it in writing. Any owner looking to buy into the NFL, or the NBA, or the NHL, or major league baseball, should be willing to do the same. Put it in writing or get out of the line, and we find somebody else who is willing to commit to our city. Commit to us. Kraft sounds like a cornball, but he happens to be right, he is the caretaker of a trust; these aren't dry-cleaning franchises or fast-food joints or used-car dealerships. He is honest enough to know that no matter how much of his money he put up to get the Patriots, the team still belongs to the fans he visits in the parking lots around the stadium every Sunday, shaking hands, talking to them, listening to them.

We are not just customers to people like Kraft.

We are his partners.

We don't expect these owners, most of whom wouldn't be caught dead sitting in an end-zone seat in December, or sitting in baseball's bleachers on some cold nowhere night in September watching a team going nowhere, ever to love us back. We know they are full of it when they say they do. But there has to come a time in sports when there is a law on the books saying that when you're done going through the fans' pockets in Cleveland, you are not allowed to go off and do the same thing in Baltimore.

So make them sign a prenup. With no loopholes about their leases or their stadiums, no contingencies, no deals signed in the middle of the night. No way out for people like Bill Bidwill, Georgia Frontiere, Art Modell, people to whom you wouldn't entrust ownership of a car wash.

Make them understand one thing about their team: Try to move it, you lose it.

Chapter Two

OLD DOGS, OLD TRICKS

"We can't hopscotch franchises around the country. We have built this business on the trust of the fans. If we treat them as if it doesn't count, it isn't going to wash."

—*Art Modell,*
explaining his opposition
to the Rams' move to St. Louis

You'll notice I mentioned Art Modell only in passing in the last chapter. That's because I feel he deserves a chapter all his own.

This is how you lose your team:

On the night of October 27, 1995, at somewhere around 30,000 feet, Art Modell finally bailed himself out of the $60 million hole he said he'd dug for himself running the Cleveland Browns. He sold them, and himself, to Baltimore. He did this at about the exact same time the Cleveland Indians baseball team was in the process of losing the World Series to the Atlanta Braves.

As far as anyone knew, this was the first time one city had lost both a Series and a football team in the same night.

The symbolism of Modell, who'd always lived high and seen himself as some kind of celebrity, making his deal while in midair seemed perfect. So that is where he sold the Browns and sold out Cleveland. He was on a private jet with Parris Glendening, the governor of Maryland, and a man named John Moag, head of the Maryland Sports Authority. Modell's son, David, was also on the plane. It was such an emotional moment for all of them that David Modell spilled milk on Parris Glendening's shoes.

No one cried over it.

They were frankly too busy laughing their asses off, and congratulating themselves on being high rollers that night, top guns up there in the night sky. The testosterone level in the private jet was high, all these big boys high on what was Big Sports in this country in action. Shaking hands, slapping one another on the back, knowing they were going to shock the country and the sports world with their big deal when it was announced. So they laughed up in the night sky and the joke was on fans of the Browns, who had been told by Modell as recently as 1994 that he would never consider moving the team out of Cleveland.

The same Modell who had fought Georgia Frontiere's move of the Rams out of Los Angeles and into St. Louis.

Who helped write the NFL rules on relocation of franchises that he knew he was breaking by taking his team to Baltimore in the dead of the night.

Who was breaking his contract not only with the fans of Cleveland but with the city of Cleveland, because he was now breaking a lease with Cleveland Stadium that had three more years to run, basically folding that lease up into a paper airplane.

And you know why Modell was doing all this? For the same reason some old dog licks his balls.

Because he can.

Art, you old dog, you.

So now it was all out in the open and official: Even full stadiums didn't count anymore.

We knew empty stadiums sometimes got results. There was always the feeling that if enough of us stayed away, even the biggest jerk owner in the world would eventually sit up and take notice. The ticket booth wasn't a real ballot box; we still didn't have Election Day. But at least we could get the bastards' attention and sometimes even get results. The season after the Miracle Mets won the World Series in 1969, the Mets drew 2.7 million fans to Shea Stadium. By 1981, attendance was down to about 700,000, which meant that there were nearly two million missing Mets fans holed up somewhere in the tristate New York area.

Why?

Because watching the Mets in those years was about as much fun as watching open-heart surgery, that's why.

Know what happened?

The Payson family, which had owned the Mets from the beginning, quit, and sold the Mets to Fred Wilpon and Nelson Doubleday. By the end of the next decade, the Mets had won a World Series and were drawing more people to Shea than they ever had, and the whole organization was the envy of everybody else in baseball.

(Wilpon and Doubleday would make their own rockhead mistakes after that, because even the best operations can go wrong, even owners who seem to know what they're doing can start making wrong turns. But at the time this book was being written, the Mets seemed to be rebuilding. Wilpon and Doubleday were two owners who woke up before they blew the franchise.)

That World Series the Mets won in 1986 started with empty seats in 1979 and 1980 and 1981.

Full stadiums, though, are supposed to be an entirely different matter. They don't guarantee that a team will win anything. But if you go to the ticket window and pay your money and support your team, the bastards who own it aren't supposed to quit on you.

In theory, anyway.

It doesn't always work that way. The football Raiders had seen twelve straight seasons of sellouts when Al Davis up and moved them to Los Angeles. Davis couldn't get the kind of stadium deal he wanted, and he was obsessed with luxury boxes even in the early 1980s, with their potential, sure he couldn't compete with richer teams in bigger markets if he didn't have them. I thought he was right at the time, and supported his right to move his team, having bought into the Dry Cleaner Theory of sports. And I found out over time that I was dead wrong, as bubbleheaded as a sports owner.

(It was a jump ball in those days whether I was a bigger sucker for free-agent ballplayers or free-agent owners.)

Davis, by the way, never did get his new stadium in Los Angeles, ended up spending his entire time in a dump called the Los Angeles Coliseum, and finally went back to Oakland when Oakland gave him all the stadium improvements and luxury boxes and dough he couldn't get in 1983.

Who has more fun than a sports owner?

Davis walked out on twelve seasons of sellouts. Modell walked away on thirty years of sellouts, and television money, and concessions, and all the rest of it. And when he did, here is what one of his fellow owners said about him:

"If I had owned the Cleveland Browns as long as he has, not only would I not be in the hole this sonofabitch says he is in, I'd own a team in every sport. This guy has fucked up one of the great cash cows, no matter how much he's trying to plead poverty now. And even after the way he's fucked it up over such a long period of time, guess what? He's still talking about a business that's worth at least $200 million on the open market."

Two hundred million.

Would you care to guess how much of his own money Modell put up to buy the team in 1962?

Two hundred and fifty thousand.

But Modell wasn't going to sell. Sell? Are you nuts? Without his team, he was back to being a nobody. And nobody would have cared how much funding he had done to the arts in Cleveland, or to charity. He thought he was the Browns. He liked the way people sucked around him because of that. It is the same with so many of these guys. Without the Yankees, George Steinbrenner was just another shipbuilder. And a second-rate shipbuilder at that. Steinbrenner's company was known as American Shipbuilding. If you're looking for it, try the bottom of Tampa Bay. He did about as well with ships in the 1980s as he did with bats and balls.

Sell? Modell and Steinbrenner would sell a kidney before they would sell their teams.

When Modell first announced the move to Baltimore, he blubbered about how he had to do it for his family, as if he were Grandpa Walton trying to secure John-Boy's future. Even Al Davis, who opened the door for Modell by moving the Raiders up and down the California coast, sneered.

"What," Davis said a few days later, "his goddamn family didn't matter before?"

(Owners have all the qualities of dogs except loyalty. Please remember that Modell was only doing to Cleveland what Davis had done to both Oakland and Los Angeles.)

Modell, that slob, didn't just whine about his family. He also whined that Cleveland had built a new stadium for the Indians, a new arena for the Cavaliers of the NBA, even had finally built the Rock and Roll Hall of Fame while he was waiting for them to take care of him. But the truth is, he was the one conducting a bad-faith negotiation with the mayor of Cleveland and with everybody else involved in something that would have looked like slapstick when it was all over, if he hadn't pissed all over the rights of some of the best fans anywhere in sports.

Didn't matter to Modell.

If he was going to look like a whore in front of the whole world, he wanted to look like one with a heart of gold. And maybe he didn't care one way or the other once he got his money.

By then, he looked like a whore who'd inherited the whole mine.

What Modell did to Cleveland was just a variation of a hustle that had been going on in Big Sports for a long time, all the way back to Ebbets Field. And in the end, everybody except the fans in Cleveland got what they wanted:

Paul Tagliabue stayed out of court with Modell and the state of Maryland, which was just fine with the NFL commissioner, who has the kind of phobia about courtrooms that some people have about flying.

Baltimore got a team.

Cleveland mayor Michael White cut a deal with Tagliabue and the league that guaranteed his city a team by 1999. He also got the league to agree to help finance a new stadium for that new team. So White kept alive his own ambitions of running either for governor or senator in Ohio.

Modell didn't just get his money, he got cheered every time he set foot in Baltimore.

Browns fans? They got a real good screwing from every single party involved. And were told to like it. Not just to like it, but be grateful for it. Oh, sure. Please take a look at how it was presented to them, by both the league and their own politicians:

They were supposed to put on party hats and start blowing noisemakers because they didn't get it nearly as badly as Baltimore got it when it had lost the Colts. That is why Modell's fellow owners nearly tore rotator cuffs patting themselves on the back. And no one wanted to point out that these were the same people who had voted against giving Baltimore an expansion team in 1993. That's why it isn't just Modell, it is all of them. It is a whole parliament of whores. Which is a little insulting to people in government. Compared to sports, government is like church.

When the whole thing was over, Tagliabue even admitted that the NFL never actually determined if the Browns met the league's criteria for leaving one city for another. He talked about how the league would be maintaining tradition in Cleveland by keeping the name "Browns" there, and all the Browns' records. Right. It is as if Steinbrenner moved the Yankees out of Yankee Stadium, and baseball passed a rule that he couldn't have the "NY" logo, he couldn't keep the pin-striped uniforms, and the next team into Yankee Stadium got all of Babe Ruth's home runs.

But Tagliabue talked about tradition with a straight face (it's really the only one he has). Modell did the exact same thing every time they'd stick a microphone in front of his perpetually sad, puffy face in Baltimore.

"There's a tremendous tradition here," Modell said to the cheering masses. "Great football fans. The Modell family, and associates, are happy to be a part of it."

Happier than a pig in you-know-what.

You want the best postscript of all on the Browns' move to Baltimore? It came from Alex Spanos, owner of the San Diego Chargers.

The vote on the Browns had been held. Despite all the tough talk going on, only Ralph Wilson of the Buffalo Bills and Dan

Rooney of the Pittsburgh Steelers had voted against Modell. Wilson and Modell have been friends for years, but the Bills' owner—who has been every bit the football success that Modell has been an old fool—delivered a forty-five-minute speech, to Modell and the room, about the mistake he felt the league was making.

Wilson, a quiet, dignified man, finally looked Modell in the eye and said, "We cannot treat our customers this way. Doing this to your fans is the same as doing it to my fans, and Dan's, and everybody else's."

Again: Ralph Wilson couldn't stop Modell, and neither could Tagliabue, and neither could a binding lease. Everybody knew it going in. All the rhetoric—even the kind of passionate rhetoric that Wilson offered at a conference room at an airport hotel in Chicago, the kind of thetoric we hardly ever get from the people who run sports—finally just became part of the hustle. The hustle that ended with the people of Cleveland being told that the whole shabby episode was a Good Thing.

When the meeting was over, Wilson came out to talk to the media. So did Modell. So did Alex Spanos, bless his heart.

"I don't like all this moving that's going on," Spanos said gravely.

Then he paused and looked straight at the camera and said, "But it sure does pay off."

There are days in sports when we hate them all.

KEITH OLBERMANN

Keith Olbermann has worked in both television and radio for nearly twenty years. Since March of 1992, he has been with ESPN, where, along with Dan Patrick, he usually hosts the hour-long version of *SportsCenter.* He is one of the best writers working anywhere in television at this time. At a time in sports when there are so few distinctive voices, Olbermann has one. I said to him, as I said to some other smart friends from sports whose voices will appear in this book: "Say you're king of the world. Give me one thing to make the whole thing better." His reply:

You want a couple of magic bullets to fix sports? Here are two:

1. From January 1 in the year after the approval of this amendment to the Constitution of the United States, any official of any government, state, or city who pays, suggests his government should pay, or promises a sports franchise or any single voter that it will pay, money towards building the franchise a stadium or remodeling an existing one, that official will be sentenced to a life at hard labor in a federal penitentiary. (Hey, these are drastic times, and drastic times call for drastic measures, right?)

The benefits of this law would be manifold. Instantaneously, we would see blessed relief from the ethics-resistant business mutation to which owners euphemistically refer to as "franchise free agency" but is in fact franchise blackmail. Eliminate politicians who buy votes by buying teams and you will restore the free market to sports leagues.

Want to move?

Pay for it yourself.

Want to replace a bad facility?

Pay for it yourself.

There would also be several lesser benefits, foremost of them the chance to preserve our historical ballparks rather than take the easy route of replacing them with publicly financed soulless dumps. Since 1990, we've lost Comiskey Park and Boston Garden solely because cash was stolen from community coffers. Tiger Stadium could be next. Then Fenway Park, Maple Leaf Gardens, you name it.

Pass this law, and a complete overhaul of Yankee Stadium would consist of a fresh coat of paint—and George Steinbrenner would have to be happy about it.

Perhaps the best and most unexpected side effect here would be the resultant forced return of fiscal responsibility to many spendthrift franchises. If you can't count on Uncle Nashville to bail you out, you might actually parcel out your salaries a little more deftly.

Oh, and by the way, the fan would benefit from this, because his or her city might just spend that sports subsidy money on, well, real life. As a Stanford economist wrote in the Times *last month about New York's proposed investment in a new Yankee facility, New York would make more money by just putting the cash in a savings account.*

2. Any player in any sport who intentionally makes serious physical contact with a referee, umpire, or other league-assigned official shall be suspended for one year without pay.

Very simple one here.

In 1945, catcher Charlie "Greek" George of the Philadelphia A's, disagreeing with a call by home-plate umpire Joe Rue, turned around and socked Rue in the jaw. George was promptly banned for life. There hasn't been a baseball umpire punched by a major leaguer since.

Chapter Three

GOVERNORS, MAYORS, AND OTHER SPORTS PIMPS

We need a Code of Conduct for owners.

Especially when one of them shows up with a hand out, wanting a new stadium or new arena.

No matter how bad a boy or girl they've been.

Now there are economists all over the map who will tell you that the biggest scam in Big Sports in the new-stadium hustle. A scam that goes on all the time, by the way, in cities all over North America:

Team owner says he can't compete in current facility, which he describes as being something that wouldn't qualify for public housing. Says he needs a new one, will leave if he doesn't get one. Looks needier than a panhandler.

At this point the mayor of your city and the governor of your state start falling all over themselves to help the guy out.

Only they aren't reaching into their pockets, they're reaching into yours.

Before you know it, they have produced a zillion-dollar plan to keep the team in town, build a new facility for it, allow—or so they say—everyone to live happily every after. Because—they say—if we lose the White Sox/Pirates/Brewers to St. Petersburg/northern Virginia/Charlotte, the quality of life in Chicago/Pittsburgh/Milwaukee will never be the same, and if you don't believe that, look at the way Brooklyn never really recovered its complete civic identity after Walter O'Malley moved the Dodgers west. After O'Malley, way back in the 1950s, didn't get the kind of new-stadium deal in Brooklyn that he was after.

Sports owners may be dumb, but are never as dumb as a politician.

You can also tape that one to the refrigerator door when you're trying to figure how the whole thing got away from us.

Somehow politicians in this country have been convinced that buying an owner a new park is the same as buying him a brand-new set of brains.

And most economists, when they look at the cost of building the thing and the cost to the constituency, say it is a crock as tall as the tallest point in your existing ballpark. That is just an element in the outdated and unrealistic romance we still attach to sports, despite all the times that sports has screwed us over, and sometimes screwed us over royally.

"We've got cities that are now held hostage by professional sports teams," the economist Rob Baade says. "Cities that are told, if you don't build a better facility, one that can generate more revenue through luxury seating, then maybe the team will look for greener pastures."

The greener pastures absolutely littered with luxury seating, as far as the eye can see, luxury seating and private boxes and food courts so plentiful and diverse you can miss half a game deciding what you want to eat.

What Baade and others like him are really saying to us, all the fans who are asked over and over again to sign off on these deals, is this: Listen, schmucks, don't trust the mayor and don't trust the governor, because they take the recreation dollars the owner of the team hasn't taken already.

In the end, the sports fan feels as if his payout schedule to his team is more regular than alimony. Because after we have paid and paid to support loser owners and loser teams, here come the politicians with grand schemes for new taxes or schemes financed by casino taxes in states in which gambling is legal, or schemes floating on top of municipal bonds, like clouds floating on blue skies on sunny days. They want us to believe that voting for these schemes is the same as voting a World Series team or Super Bowl team or NBA champion into office. It doesn't work that way, of course, even as the building boom goes on. And it goes on and on. In Big Sports, the 1980s never really ended. American cities spent $750 million in the '80s to renovate existing stadiums and arenas, or build new ones. Now there is the feeling that by the time the '90s are over, the cost will be at least $5 billion and maybe as high as $10 billion.

You see what is happening here: The price of the park has gotten as outrageous as the price of the ballplayers playing in it.

It really is a beautiful thing. And no one stops it. As the economists keep screaming that this is nuts, that what we are seeing is the politicians act even crazier about sports than the craziest sports fan, there are sensible people from government who say that sports is worth this kind of money, that you have to do whatever it takes to keep your team. One such politician is Mario Cuomo, the ex-governor of New York State, and a man who, while still in office, led the fight to keep the Yankees in New York City rather than risk losing them to New Jersey—the state had already lost the Giants and Jets to Giants Stadium in the New Jersey Meadowlands—or even to Tampa, owner George Steinbrenner's home.

"Let me ask you something," Cuomo says. "When was the last time you saw an economist driving a BMW?"

Cuomo smiles. Why not? He's out of politics now, practicing law and hosting a nationally syndicated radio show. He is out of the business of selling people who live in his city and his state on a $1 billion plan to move the Yankees out of Yankee Stadium and into new digs on the Lower West Side of Manhattan. It means Cuomo is also out of the business of selling what is only a sweetheart deal to one person—Steinbrenner, the Yankee owner—as the best thing to happen in New York since the Yankees got Babe Ruth from the Red Sox for $100,000.

"Economists are always wrong," Cuomo says. "Their lives are all about extravagant, elegant bullshit."

I point out to Cuomo that Steinbrenner and all the other sports owners have always survived on the exact same extravagant and elegant excrement.

Politicans, too.

"You cannot just use numbers to justify the cost of sports," Cuomo says. "You can't do it with the stadium any more than you can do it with the salaries you hear the players are making. If you try to make the numbers in sports add up, you'll drive yourself crazy."

It sounds like part of the hustle, too, even coming from someone as brilliant, and decent, as Cuomo. Politicans know they can't justify what they want to pay to hold on to teams, the blackmail they have to pay to owners to keep them in town. Owners know they can't justify what they pay to their ballplayers. Television networks, in the end, can't justify what they pay to sports leagues. But *we* are supposed to accept higher taxes and higher ticket prices, like the good soldiers that we are, and we are supposed to do that every single time we are asked. Nobody really gives a damn about justifying our numbers. The owners just know this: They want what they want when they want it. Same with the players. And we have this feeling, more and more, that we are watching these players and these games with some kind of meter running.

Every time there is a commercial break, we feel as if we should hear the ka-ching of another cash register.

Someday our new color television set will come equipped with the kind of slot you see at the gas station, so we can keep running our credit card through.

When I first talked to Cuomo about the plan to move the Yankees, he estimated that the final cost would be around $850 million. Two weeks later, when the story hit the papers, New York City mayor Rudolph Giuliani was talking about the whole thing being all the way up to that $1 billion figure. Maybe more. At least the mayor was catching on fast to how Big Sports works in this country. New Yorkers were just being reminded all over again, and finding out that ballparks can sometimes remind us of ballplayers: The cost of them sometimes goes up before they've ever done anything.

"Is the new place worth that much?" Cuomo asks. "Are the Yankees worth that much to the city and the state? Obviously, I've always thought they are. But if you are asking me to prove it with numbers—the way the economists say they can prove the Yankees aren't worth it—I can't do that. Because how much is goodwill worth? Ultimately, there is no way of measuring that, or measuring the exact amount of money, over the long haul, that you will make in added tourism by keeping the ballclub in your city, your state. Is there a lot of romance involved here? You bet there is. Is some of the romance bullshit, too? Sure it is.

"Do I believe that New York should municipally finance a new stadium for this man? I don't. I believe that the only way to get this done is with an awful lot of private financing, which is always tricky. But having told you all that, I would still try to keep the Yankees. Because I believe they will, over all the years, pay for this thing. Because it is good for the image of the city. And its vanity. At the end of the day, you attract money to sports because of vanity: my vanity, your vanity, everybody's. Having the Yankees stay in New York is a good thing."

So it is a Good Thing in New York when somebody has to come up, one way or the other, with a billion dollars.

But it was a Good Thing in Cleveland, or so they were told by the National Football League, when their politicians didn't come up with the money it would have cost them to keep the Browns.

It was a Good Thing for the Indians to get Jacobs Field in Cleveland, a ballpark that can now be sold out for an entire season before that baseball season begins, even at a time when the Cleveland school system is in receivership.

Don't worry, be happy.

At the same time Steinbrenner says he needs a new stadium in New York, Bug Selig of the Milwaukee Brewers says he needs a new one in Milwaukee. Selig is right about that. His ballpark, County Stadium, has been one of the dumps of sports for years, and he doesn't want to see the Brewers leave Milwaukee the way the Braves did when Selig was a kid. So he wants a new park, with a retractable roof, because there are whole big chunks of the baseball season when playing baseball in Milwaukee is the same as playing it in the Yukon.

You turn on the television set to watch a Brewers game in April or May, and you half expect to see the lead dogs in the Iditarod come plowing through the place.

But because the Indians have gotten to be a formidable team again in their new ballpark, and the Colorado Rockies, an expansion team playing in lovely ballpark digs called Coors Field, made the playoffs in only their third season, the implication is that Selig will then have a real team to put inside his new park. Remember the drill here: good ballpark, good team to follow, even though the Brewers haven't been in a World Series since 1982 and have done nothing for years, on the field or in Selig's front office, to indicate that is going to change anytime soon.

Selig, though, is pure of heart in a couple of ways. First, he wants to keep his team in Milwaukee. "I grew up with the Milwaukee Braves," Selig says, "and had my heart broken when they moved to Atlanta, and kept having my heart broken every time Henry Aaron hit a home run as an Atlanta Brave." So Selig does not want to go off to Charlotte, where they are sweatier with lust than Baltimore was for the Browns. But he can only stay if he gets one of those flip-top-box parks like the Blue Jays have at SkyDome.

Cost? Two hundred and fifty million.

But here is where Selig is not just pure of heart, he comes up looking like a hero, especially when you put him up against his fellow owners, the ones who have new ballparks and the ones looking to get them. Because as this book was being written, Bud Selig was still trying to do something that most sports owners wouldn't do if you pulled a gun on them:

Raise some of the money for a new stadium himself.

Praise the Lord and pass the collection plate.

SO WHAT DO WE DO?: I

Here is the first bylaw in our Code of Conduct for owners:

If they want a new stadium, if they say that a new stadium is all that can keep them in town and keep them going, first they have to be willing to finance 25 percent of it themselves.

Or 20 percent.

Or 15 percent.

I'm willing to negotiate here.

This can all be part of the prenup agreement about keeping the team right where it is. If somebody needs help to stay, if he really does need a new ballpark or arena to survive, he has a perfect right to ask his city and his state to give him a hand.

But first he's got to show us the color of his money.

An owner has to reach into his own pocket for a change. Or her own pocket. Walter O'Malley will always be the most hated man in Brooklyn history, and maybe he was always intending to go west, but before he did, he at least tried to build a new park for himself in Brooklyn to replace Ebbets Field. And O'Malley was willing to put up some of his own money. The Baruch College economist Neil Sullivan, who wrote *The Dodgers Move West*, tells in that book of how O'Malley wanted to buy land and build his new Ebbets Field on Atlantic Avenue in Brooklyn. The City of New York instead offered him a new stadium in Flushing Meadows, Queens (eventually it would be the site of Shea Stadium, now the home of the New York Mets . . . until the Mets get their new retractable-roof stadium nearby). O'Malley chose not to be a tenant in what he called "a political ballpark."

As if there is any other kind of ballpark.

Then or now.

So O'Malley went out and got the kind of sweetheart land deal and lease deal in downtown Los Angeles that all the other teams in all the other sports have been looking for, in some form or fashion, ever since. Before existing ballparks, even domed stadiums, reach the age of twenty-five, the big daddy who owns them wants another one. We are supposed to give it to them, or the deal is always the same: The next thing we see is taillights from the back of the moving van.

But if we do give it to them—we the fans, we the taxpayers—we want to be partners in at least this one area of sports. We should be able to do what everybody was trying to do in Milwaukee, Wisconsin: at least make the whole thing a partnership between the owners and the taxpayers. The state was willing to put up $160 million if Selig could come up with $90 million of his own.

The state raises taxes a little—in the case of this stadium plan, a one-tenth of one percent sales-tax in the eight counties—and Selig does the rest. For all the crimes I believe Selig helped commit leading up to the baseball strike of 1994, and then during it, he has gone about this exactly right as a way of keeping his ballclub at home. He does not want to move. He does not want to sell. He also does not think that even in his sport's smallest market, he is on some kind of lifetime scholarship because he has the Brewers. The Brewers have never made much money, so Selig has never come at this with some kind of dumb-ass Richie Rich mentality about how sports should work.

"I believe the only way this sort of thing really works," Selig says, "is with a public and private partnership. I think it's incumbent upon any owner who says he needs a new stadium to be willing to enter into a partnership like this. This was a deal I felt obligated to make."

Selig has lost money, and for a long time, on his losing teams. Steinbrenner, on the other hand, has done nothing but make money with the Yankees. He put up around eight million of his own to buy them; now the team could be worth $300 million, maybe more, if he ever put it up for sale, as Yankees fans fervently hope he will someday. He is still in the middle of a television deal with the Madison Square Garden network in New York that pays him around $50 million a year in rights fees. That is before he ever opens the doors to his ballpark or sells a ticket. He whines about Yankee Stadium all the time, about the Bronx neighborhood that is the team's address and has been since Babe Ruth, whines that he does not have luxury boxes. But he has occasionally gone years without paying the city of New York the rent money he owes them on his current lease.

He says the city hasn't lived up to its end of the lease, and always cites the fact that the city hasn't given him the parking spaces to which he is entitled (sometimes the sense of entitlement from owners makes even ballplayers look more grateful than a televangelist at telethon time). The city lets him get away with it. Because the city doesn't want to make him mad.

So of course he just keeps asking for more.

But the first thing this creep should have to do if he wants a new Yankee Stadium is write a check. Pay his fair share. Selig was looking to raise that 36 percent in Milwaukee, but we'll give Steinbrenner a break. We won't ask him for $360 million toward a new Yankee Stadium.

Two hundred and fifty million ought to do it.

If he doesn't want to pay, then he can explain to his fans why he never has to pony up any dough every time he wants a new Yankee Stadium. Steinbrenner, a lifetime phony, might be funnier doing that than he ever was on *Seinfeld*.

SO WHAT DO WE DO?: II

Here is the second bylaw in our Code of Conduct for owners:

Three strikes and you're out.

Let me explain.

Less than two months into the 1996 baseball season, Marge Schott was at it again.

It wasn't a dead umpire getting her into trouble this time, it was a dead Nazi.

Schott went on ESPN and talked about how Hitler hadn't been such a bad guy, just a little crazy at the end.

About a week later, Schott was in *Sports Illustrated* magazine making disparaging remarks about Asian-Americans coming to this country and taking "our" jobs.

So she got punished, had to give up day-to-day operations of the Reds.

That made two suspensions.

Schott was as much a threat to whatever integrity baseball had left as the Cleveland Indians' Albert Belle was at the exact same time for his own pattern of rockheaded behavior. Schott seemed hellbent on offending every ethnic and racial group there is, not to mention the entire homosexual community. Belle? He seemed ready to lash out with his own thuggish behavior at anyone who got in his way. Sometimes the punks of sports range from home-run-hitting African-Americans to rich old white women.

Ballplayers never get disciplined properly. Maybe we can at least start with the owners. There should be a machinery in place that if Schott gets suspended a third time, if George Steinbrenner gets suspended a third time, then she or he is out of the game for good.

Three strikes and you're out.

Right away, people will jump up and scream, "This is America. You can't force someone to sell a business."

Except that owning a sports team isn't like owning another business—we've gone over this before. It's like being a member of a cartel. If you don't like the word cartel, just think of people like Schott as being members of a very exclusive country club. Country clubs make their own rules.

I asked David Stern one time about the owners in the NBA, how hard it is for him to keep his schmucks in line.

"You've got the wrong guy," Stern said.

"Seriously," I said. "What's your schmuck quotient?"

"Don't have one. Even if I did admit there was such a thing as a Schmuck Quotient," he said, "I have to be honest, in this league it's very, very low. Are all my owners perfect? Of course they're not. Do they piss off the commissioner sometimes? You bet they do. But for the most part, I've got good guys. You don't have a chance to be a good commissioner without good guys, believe me."

So Stern doesn't have a lot of teams looking to move. He doesn't have schmucks like Modell or Marge Schott. So it really is much easier for him to be a genius commissioner. He keeps his guys in line. Gary Bettman of the National Hockey League keeps his guys in line. Peter Rozelle used to do it in the National Football League. For a while, it looked as if Paul Tagliabue was doing the same thing, until all holy hell broke loose the last couple of years, and now Tagliabue has a bunch of rules about franchise location that he can fold up into a party hat. It is why Tagliabue spent so much of his time in early 1996 explaining why the Cleveland Browns could move to Baltimore and the Houston Oilers could move to Nashville, but he wanted the Seattle Seahawks to stay in Seattle and not move to Los Angeles.

And even if Stern or Bettman or Tagliabue had Marge Schott, maybe they wouldn't be able to do anything with her, either. Even the best commissioners are hired by the owners. And work for the owners. Maybe no owner wants to put any real teeth into rules governing behavior and conduct, because he/she is afraid those same rules will come back to bite him/her someday.

One of these days, everyone will realize that a commissioner should be hired by both the owners and the players, that there should be some kind of supreme council in each sport composed equally of ownership people and union people, and they will all get together and pick The Man. The owners would pay half the commissioner's salary and the union would pay half. He would have to answer to both of them. If the baseball owners can get together and whack out Fay Vincent, which they did, the same thing could happen someday to either Stern or Bettman or Tagliabue. No one is saying it will. But no one thought the commissioner of baseball would ever be fired, either.

Stern has all the power in the world because his owners, devoid of the Schmuck Quotient, or so he says, bestow that power on him. And he makes them piles of money. And basketball keeps growing all the time, not just in this country but all over the world. But if there came the day in pro basketball when the sport was being rocked by one scandal after another, when there was, say, the perception that half the league was on drugs—and that was the perception at the end of the 1970s—and profits started to fall and television ratings started to drop faster than George Bush's approval rating did between the Gulf War and Bill Clinton, then David Stern would be gone. He'd be rich. He'd go down in basketball history as the man who was in charge during an incredible boom period.

He'd be gone.

The owners would still be there.

Schmucks or otherwise.

The only way we get rid of an owner is when he/she decides to sell. And as I have been telling you, that only happens as a last resort. And that is the reason why we need more teams in sports like the Green Bay Packers. The Packers? Yes, which leads us to . . .

SO WHAT DO WE DO?: III

Of all the solutions that have been offered here, the very best solution would be to have more operations like the one they have in Green Bay.

Because the Packers are owned by the fans.

By us.

Accountable to us.

Forget about a bunch of rich NBA zillionaries going to the Summer Games every four years and kicking ass on all the underdeveloped basketball nations. The Packers are the real Dream Team. At a time when too much is wrong with sports, the Packers are one of the things that is right.

Even if she did somehow end up running the Packers, someone

like Marge Schott would be out of there by the next board of directors meeting if she embarrassed her team and her sport.

(You know who should know that better than anyone in Schott's current sport, by the way? Bud Selig. He's a member of the Packers' board of directors. Selig knows that in a time when only teams from great big markets are supposed to succeed and make money, at a time when owners now believe they are stars, a place where sports works best is a small town in Wisconsin.)

The Green Bay Packers began playing football in 1919, which means they were playing before there was even such a thing as the National Football League. But as long as there has been a National Football League, there has been a team in Green Bay, a city of 96,000. That means there has been a continuous NFL presence in Green Bay, even if the same can't be said of St. Louis or Baltimore or Los Angeles.

Or Cleveland.

Back in the 1920s, there were forty-nine different cities sponsoring NFL franchises, including Kenosha, Racine, Canton, Dayton, Akron, Evansville, Marion, and Duluth. Of all those smaller cities, only Green Bay has survived as a home to a major—and storied—professional franchise.

In 1994, even before the Packers made it back to the January 1996 NFC championship game against the Cowboys, *Money* magazine rated the Packers the second-best buy for sports fans. First was the Cowboys. The ratings in *Money* were based on several criteria: availability and cost of parking, access to public transportation, availability of good seats and their cost, the cleanliness of the stadium, the behavior of the crowd, the cost of concessions, the quality of the team's performance, the appeal of its stars.

By 1995, a total of 4,632 shares of Packer stock had been sold. The team had 1,877 shareholders. Forty-five private citizens sit on the board of directors. Seven serve on the executive committee.

Chief executives of the Packers have included Bob Harlan, a long-time Packer administrator; a real estate salesman; a retired judge. Former Packers players such as Willie Davis and Jim Temp serve on the board of directors. As of two years ago, even after signing a rich football free agent Reggie White for $17 million in 1993, the Packers had $22 million in the bank, accruing interest every single day.

The Packers were established as a nonprofit organization in 1922, which means that the stockholders do not receive dividends. So the Packers, like old Eliot Ness of "The Untouchables," cannot be bought. Maybe they are the one thing of true value left in sports at this time that cannot be bought. Packers stock is valued at a constant $25. Until the 1960s, when the NFL decided to share its television dividends among the franchises, the Packers were basically kept afloat by the generosity of its fans.

A team by the people.

And for the people.

In the real world, a system like this could work only in pro football, with a plan of revenue-sharing that starts everybody off with about $40 million every season. But isn't it pretty to think that it could work everywhere, big markets and small markets, all over the map?

Oh, there are luxury boxes in Green Bay, the way there are luxury boxes everywhere else. The Packers do not live in the past. There are 198 luxury boxes at Green Bay's Lambeau Field, and there is a 1,500-person waiting list to get them. Games have basically been sold out there for the last forty years.

All of this started back in '22, when old Curly Lambeau sold his car for $250 to buy the Packers a place in pro football.

What does this mean?

It means there is a place where someone like Schott could never rule. No Jerry Joneses in Green Bay, no Steinbrenners. No Modells. The *Sporting News* once described the Packers as a fantasy team come to life. And what does it all mean? It means that when an owner does put a team up for sale in this country, in any sport, the first thing he must do is make a public offering.

Before the next Schott or Jones or Steinbrenner comes along.

Put that in the Code of Conduct for owners, too.

Put it up real high.

Last January, I was standing with Fuzzy Thurston, the tough old offensive lineman from Lombardi's Packers, a football legend who has turned out to be even tougher since he stopped playing football. Thurston has had a hip replaced, and has survived throat-cancer surgery. He owns a bar in Green Bay called Shenanigans, and the place is a link between the Packers' charming, successful present and its glorious past. Thurston presides over it all.

And he still travels to the big games. So he had come to watch the Packers try to make it back to the Super Bowl for the first time since Lombardi. He looked around Texas Stadium, with all its Nike advertising, all its garish Texas excess, and smiled. Because of his surgery, speaking can be difficult for Thurston.

A wonderful sense of perspective about sports comes quite easily to him. Maybe it is because of his frame of reference. Not just Lombardi. But Green Bay, Wisconsin.

"They call these guys here America's Team," Thurston said. "Bullshit. The Packers are America's Team."

The next time a For Sale sign goes up on one of these teams, all the wonder-boy commissioners ought to keep that in mind.

People aren't mad as hell in Green Bay. They want their team to win and they get as sad as anybody else in sports when some young talent like Brett Favre, the team's star quarterback, the NFC's Most Valuable Player for the 1995 season, checks into rehab because of an addiction to painkillers, trailed into rehab by rumors on ESPN that he would be treated for a drinking problem as well. So Green Bay is not bulletproof, either.

It turns out that in Big Sports the best place of all is smallest. A team with less money in the bank than Michael Jordan.

SO WHAT DO WE DO?: IV

Sometimes the best you can do with rat owners—in baseball especially, where teams hardly ever move these days—is hit them with economic sanctions.

Then hope they shut up and get out, the way Tom Werner did.

Some people stay away from the games. Others don't want to do that. A lot of fans boycotted Reds games in Cincinnati during the 1995 season, which is why there were so many empty seats during the playoffs. But some people don't want to do that, because they will want their games, even if their ticket money goes to the rat owner. But there are other ways to cut into an owner's profits. They require a little effort, and a little work, but again: You can't go around bitching about the way things are if you're not willing to even throw a few jabs at the Big Daddy owners.

So park a few blocks farther away from the ballpark, so the team doesn't get your parking money. Let the club keep your ticket money—you want to see your team, you're not willing to give up the games.

Just hold back the five bucks or ten bucks they charge you to park your car.

And bring your own food. I know, you don't want to turn a trip to the ballpark into Outward Bound. If you wanted to go on a picnic, you'd go on a picnic. But if you want to take back the seats, if you want to do what you can to run off an idiot and oppressive owner, you do what you can. Professional sports teams need their ticket revenue and they need their television revenue, both locally and from the networks. They also need the money they gouge out of you for a hot dog, a soft drink, a beer, ice cream.

Don't give it to them, whether you are a season-ticket holder or just someone who goes to five or ten games a year.

It's like they tell you in the advertising for state lotteries:

You can't win it if you're not in it.

Other Voices

GLENN (DOC) RIVERS

Doc Rivers, who started out with the Atlanta Hawks, played the 1995–96 season with the San Antonio Spurs. At the end of that season Rivers—one of the best guys I have ever known in sports—took a job as an NBA television analyst for TNT. When I said to him, "Give me one thing to make the whole thing better," this is what he said:

Fix Number one: All Weekday games in the NBA start no later than 6:30 P.M. All weekend games can start no later than 5:30 P.M. Why? Because we are raising an entire generation of kids who aren't ever going to see us play a second half, because in this country the second half is now past their bedtimes.

Fix Number Two: Each kid with a ticket who is under the age of fourteen gets a sandwich and a drink for one-half off the normal price.

It's crazy that a family outing in sports now costs as much as it does, plain and simple.

Fix Number Three: Let's have a toll-free number like this—1-800-WIN-A-LOT.

With this system, ticket prices would be directly tied into a team's win-loss record. Make up the formula you think is right. Let's say 75 percent to the home team, 25 percent to the visitors. Season-ticket holders get a rebate if their team underperforms. But prices go up on single-game tickets if a team does better than expected. (Prices could even vary on a game-to-game basis.)

Example: Chicago wins 72 games, or Seattle wins 64 games. In those cities you would have to pay a premium cost for tickets.

Say Chicago, on its way to 72 wins, plays a team like the 76ers, on their way to winning only 25. If Chicago is the home team, cost would still be high. Why? Because fans are willing to pay for success, even perfection. If the Bulls went into Philadelphia, the home-team prices would be more than normal because Chicago is the opponent, but not as much as they would be in Chicago.

If two lousy teams like the 76ers and Nets get together, it wouldn't matter where the game was played, ticket prices would be real low. Maybe then we could get more kids to the game (but only if we start them when I want to start them).

Pick a week in the summer when fans will be allowed to vote on how many wins they think their team will get in the upcoming season. Their vote along with management's vote are added up, and divided by two. The number is published in the newspaper. The first twenty-five games set standard prices for season-ticket holders and single-game buyers. At that point, prices go on a week-to-week basis.

This plan would do several things: It gets the season-ticket holder base up, because it's really a no-lose situation for people with season tickets. If the team does better than expected, ticket prices will go up, but not for the ones who invested in their team early by buying season tickets. They already have their tickets at the preseason cost. If the team is doing worse than expected and prices go lower, the ones with season tickets get their rebate. Basically, this encourages the fan to buy early. I think it would make the owners and the fans happy. Also, it makes each game a different cost. Think about it: Why should fans pay the same amount of money for a Bulls–Magic game as a Bulls–76ers game? Makes no sense.

I'm probably not smart enough to figure out the exact formula. But if this plan was done right, the owners could still make their profits, and the fans could believe what fans want to believe: That they have a bit of a stake in how the game comes out.

Chapter Four

CHARLIE O AND OTHER DONKEYS

One last word about owners for now, although I know you're probably getting pretty sick of the subject. But there's just so *much* to admire about these guys, isn't there?

The last word is this:

Even smart owners can turn out to be the enemy.

The best example is the late Charles O. Finley, who built the Oakland A's of the 1970s into the best baseball machine since the New York Yankees were winning five World Series in a row between 1949 and 1954. In many ways, because he was as smart about business as he was the business of baseball, the case can be made that Finley was the most important front-office figure in the sport since Branch Rickey.

And Finley wasn't just a boss, he was an owner. He was an owner with brains, vision, flair. He didn't take any crap from the other owners, or from his players, or from his managers. To have somebody like Finley have an ownership stake in sports is more unusual than greatness in the White House. If you grade Finley against the curve—either owners who were around when he owned the A's or owners who are around now—he was Albert Einstein, just with a mule named Charlie O. as his team's mascot. The mule worked better as a figure of irony. Because there was a brief, wonderful time in baseball when Finley made donkeys out of the competition.

The A's won the World Series in 1972, 1973, and 1974. Nobody has won three in a row since. And it was even more than just the winning. Twenty years later, a brilliant baseball man named Pat Gillick built the Toronto Blue Jays into back-to-back World Series champions, before moving on to his present position as general manager of the Orioles. Gillick is a quiet man, much quieter than Finley ever was, but as he began to try to build the Orioles into a champion in the spring of 1996, Gillick laid out his philosophy: "I don't just want to be good, I want to be entertaining. Sometimes we forget that our job isn't just trying to win the games, but to put on a show for the customers, every single day." Finley's A's put on a show for the customers, every single day. Sometimes good, sometimes bad, sometimes outrageous, especially off the field. One of the clichés for baseball is calling it The Show. There was never a show like Charlie Finley's A's. They were the most colorful and flamboyant sports team of the last half-century, and maybe ever.

No one was more flamboyant, or colorful, than the owner.

Finley was the first star owner in professional sports.

The sonofabitch.

Charlie Finley put owners into play, put them in the middle of the action, the way they never had been before. Bill Veeck was always a media star in whatever city he had a team, but for all of Veeck's mad genius about baseball, he was more comfortable being a promoter than anything else; in that way, Veeck always seemed more suited for boxing than baseball. Veeck won his World Series with the '48 Indians and made it to the Series with the '59 White Sox. He just didn't win the way Finley did. And he didn't win as loud. In that way, Finley's best promotion was himself.

We just didn't know at the time that Finley had invented a form of sports terrorism.

He wasn't the worst terrorist owner, not by a long shot. Just the first. He showed all the ones who would follow him how easy it was to get their names into the paper, make headlines, even if they were the ones who had to act like donkeys and mules. Nobody would ever have an act like Finley's. Not one of the blowhard owners to follow would be as smart. It didn't stop them. They wanted to be seen, and they sure wanted to be heard. And when they started turning up in the papers all the time, it was like drugs.

Believe me, crack cocaine couldn't give George Steinbrenner more of a rush to the heart—if he actually has one—than picking up one of the New York tabloids and seeing "Boss Steinbrenner" in great, big, bold screaming type on the back page.

Charlie Finley created Steinbrenner as surely as if he'd built him with a bolt in his neck.

We had met the enemy, and he was our owner. Steinbrenner, Schott, McNall, Turner. Here's another Ted Turner story. Back in the 1970s, before CNN and Jane Fonda, Turner was desperate to be noticed, and in 1976 he was trying to recruit Reggie Jackson to come play for the Braves. The whole world was after Jackson, whom Finley had traded away from the A's the year before. Jackson had finished the '76 season with the Baltimore Orioles. Now he was a free agent, the biggest and hottest name in the first free-agent bidding frenzy, and Turner had money to burn and wanted to play.

This began twenty years of sports owners chasing free agents around the way producers chase starlets.

Even though the free agents are often the ones who end up doing to the owners what the producers want to do to the starlets.

(Before they both turn around and do that to us . . .)

Turner agreed to have dinner with Jackson at Jim McMullen's

fashionable saloon on the Upper East Side of Manhattan. Turner and Jackson had never met face-to-face, but Turner said he would already have a table when Jackson arrived, and would be easy to find.

The future Man of the Year for *Time* magazine certainly was all of that. Jackson walked into the crowded front room at McMullen's and did not have to worry about finding Turner. Turner's voice found him. Suddenly, Reggie Jackson and everybody there heard this chant coming from a table in the middle of the room:

"REG-gie!"

"REG-gie!"

"REG-Gie!"

Turner. Listing a little to one side, cockeyed grin on his face. Completely unembarrassed at the spectacle he was creating. Full of liquor and himself.

"REG-gie!"

"REG-gie!"

Turner made such an impression that Jackson ended up signing with Steinbrenner instead. The rest, of course, is baseball—and New York tabloid—history. There hadn't been a marriage this tacky since Richard Burton and Elizabeth Taylor. Both Turner and Steinbrenner and all the rest who would follow, all the way to Jerry Jones of the Dallas Cowboys, had discovered that they could be covered like one of the players. The more outrageous they were, in what they said or what they did, the more coverage they got. They began to spend outrageous sums of money, and didn't worry too much about where the money was going. They said outrageous things. Because it was the only way to be in the middle of the action. The players had games. The owners had to create controversies. Suddenly, sports was being driven by this incredibly combustible mix of bigger money, bigger egos, bigger media, bigger stage.

And the explosions that have resulted sometimes feel like Chernobyl.

Chapter Five

DARE TO BE THE BEST . . . AVAILABLE

Okay, let's move on.

Money, egos, media, stage: When you're talking all that, you're not just talking about the owners, of course, you're talking about the players, too.

The money hasn't made sports better.

The ballparks and arenas are better than they've ever been in sports. There are more shops for you than you get at the mall, and you can eat like a king. Going to a ballgame isn't just going to a ballgame anymore, it's like some sort of theme-park adventure, sports as Six Flags. And even that begins to wear your ass out after a while, because of the law somebody passed that there has to be so much loud and incessant rock-and-roll music that you feel as if you're watching the game from inside a boom box.

The money just hasn't made anything other than the creature comforts appreciably better.

And in too many ways it has made everything one hell of a lot worse.

The money has made everybody richer, no question, and bully for all of them: owners, players, agents, commissioners, television guys. (Even some sportswriters, but enough about me.) There is no question that the talent level is higher than at any other time in history, and careers last longer because athletes take better care of themselves than they ever did before, just as a way of making sure they don't have to get off the gravy train until the last possible stop. But while all this keeps happening, while the revenue stream gets higher and higher, our standards get lower, especially when it comes to who is a real star and who is not.

Who is really worth the big money and who isn't.

David Cone of the New York Yankees became the highest-paid pitcher in baseball history after the 1995 season. Cone is a fine pitcher, no question, and even has a Cy Young Award to his credit. He is also a charming clubhouse figure, always accessible to media guys like me, someone who is bright, curious, pleasant. Off the field, more athletes should be like Cone. On the field, he has also won 20 games in a season—once the standard of excellence for pitchers—exactly once. That was in 1988. He has never won a game in the World Series. Despite a reputation as one of the baseball's premier big-game pitchers, his record in the postseason is 3–2, and his earned run average is 3.96, which means four runs a game. Going into the 1996 season, Cone had a lifetime record, over ten seasons in the big leagues, of 129–78. It averages out to a record of 13–8 a season. The Yankees paid him a guaranteed contract of $19 million for the next three years and would have gone higher if they had to. Cone was a free agent and the Yankees needed him to be the ace of their staff, and so they did not just treat him as an ace when they started throwing money at him, they treated him as if he were Bob Gibson. Once again, George Steinbrenner made headlines with his largesse for a free-agent pitcher.

(Sadly, before the season was two months old, Cone would make a different kind of headline in New York, because of an aneurysm discovered—in time—in his pitching shoulder. Cone had surgery in May, and both he and the Yankees were hopeful for a full recovery.)

But every time there is another one of these contracts, the standards are lowered more, and ticket prices generally go up. It is not what you do in sports anymore. Or how much. That kind of thinking's for suckers.

It's when you do it.

When Shaquille O'Neal signed his $120 million contract with the Lakers, and Alonzo Mourning and Juwan Howard signed their $100 million deals with the Miami Heat, that seemed kind of important.

Neil O'Donnell is a quarterback who has never come close to throwing 20 touchdown passes in a season for the Pittsburgh Steelers, never gotten a whiff of the Pro Bowl, never was considered one of the top quarterbacks in the league, never was considered much more than a journeyman in the middle of the pack until the 1995–96 National Football League season. O'Donnell, though, fell into one of those situations that often enable the modern athlete to end up feeling like a Rockefeller who's finally grown into his trust fund.

He was a free agent after a career year.

"You dream about this your whole career," O'Donnell said. "This is what you work for."

Not titles, not passing records.

Being an unrestricted free agent in his prime. You want the real American dream in sports at this time? There it is. Neil O'Donnell had a dream, brother, and his dream was an expired contract and great timing. That is why he is now working on a new contract with the New York Jets that will average out to $5 million a year over the next five. Even the people who like O'Donnell and think the Jets should have gone for him don't even attempt to put him with the top guys. But understand: He does not have to be the best any more than Cone has to be the best.

The trick is being the Best Available.

If you can fall into that, teams are not just willing to pay you, they are willing to overpay. Which is what happened with O'Donnell. Fans of the Jets were reminded that O'Donnell had quarterbacked the Steelers into the previous Super Bowl. He didn't win it. In fact, he handed it to the Cowboys with two of the worst passes in Super Bowl history. But O'Donnell didn't have to win that game. He probably didn't even have to play in it to get his money. That is the way things work these days. Players don't have to win in sports to end up living like kings. They don't have to sell tickets.

They barely have to make an All-star team.

There is a basketball player named Kenny Anderson, who started the 1995–96 season with the New Jersey Nets, then was traded to the Charlotte Hornets. Anderson is a point guard out of Queens, New York, from an area known as Rego Park. He went to Georgia Tech and stayed there two seasons and then the Nets made him the No. 2 pick in the draft. I thought they were smart to do it, even though Anderson was 6'1" and looked smaller than that. He was one of those magicians with the ball, and I thought he was going to be one of the great point guards for years in the NBA.

It never worked out that way in New Jersey. Anderson was hurt a lot, and hurt by the constant change of coaches with the Nets. There were some bright moments when Chuck Daly became the coach of the team, but they did not last. Anderson made one All-Star team, and that was that. His career never became what the Nets thought it would be, and faced with losing him to free agency, they finally traded him.

But before they did, Anderson was offered a new contract that would have paid him $40 million over the next six years.

Forty million.

This was from a perennial NBA loser, one of the league's joke franchises, one that sells out only when someone like Michael Jordan or Shaquille O'Neal comes to town. They offered all that money.

He turned them down. And then said all the right things. He said he felt his career was going nowhere in New Jersey and he needed a fresh start. He was out of there. People asked him if he thought he could do better than $40 million on the open market, and Anderson said he wasn't sure and didn't care.

Then he gave you the Big Lie of Big Sports:

"It isn't about the money," Kenny Anderson said.

It's what Cone said when he signed with the Yankees. It's what O'Donnell said when he signed with the Jets. It's what Pat Riley said when he turned down the $15 million contract the Knicks were offering him to stay with them, and went to Miami for a deal worth twice that, with part ownership of the Heat thrown in.

It's even what Shaquille O'Neal said after signing his $120 million contract with the Lakers after the 1995–96 NBA season.

"I'm sick of people talking about money, money, money all the time," Shaq said.

"When they say it's not about money," says George Young, the general manager of the football Giants, "it's always about money."

Remember that one, too. It's also kind of important.

So Kenny Anderson said it wasn't about money and then promptly fired his longtime agent, Richard Howell, and hired David Falk, the Washington agent who represents Michael Jordan and Patrick Ewing and a ton of the other wealthiest players in the NBA. He didn't do it because he thinks Falk has a great personality. Falk doesn't (more about him later). On the contrary, he has the charm of a pit bull. But he is also the most powerful agent in the NBA and maybe in sports, and Anderson wanted him because of that, and because of one other thing:

For all the talk about how much he needed change, how he

wanted a new beginning for his career, Kenny Anderson thought the Nets offer was . . . low!

He went around telling his friends that as good as the offer looked, the Nets had disrespected him.

How?

Because the year before, they had given Derrick Coleman a contract whose total value was $44 million.

I know what you're thinking: How could the people who run the Nets behave like such insensitive bastards?

The Nets ended up trading both of them. But before they did, they invested $44 million in one, and were willing to invest almost that much in another. Eighty million and change for two players who had never delivered fans, media attention, glamour, credibility, all the things you are supposed to be buying in sports or entertainment for that kind of money. As teammates with the New Jersey Nets, Coleman and Anderson had won the Nets no playoff series and a total of three playoff games.

And guess what? Kenny Anderson turned out to be absolutely right. That Nets' offer was low. When he became a free agent after the 95–96 season, he signed a contract with the Portland Trailblazers for $50 million.

When he did, I asked, "Kenny, do you really believe you're a $50 million ballplayer?"

Anderson paused, then answered gravely, "Yes, I do."

There was a day a few years ago, at the United States Tennis Open in New York. At the age of thirty-nine, Jimmy Connors, the first modern player to earn big money in tennis and the one who was always worth it the most, was shocking the world—and himself—by making it to the semifinals of the Open. Nothing like it in tennis had happened since Ken Rosewall had done it at the same age, at both Wimbledon and the Open in 1974. Rosewall made it to the finals of both those tournaments, then got dusted by a twenty-one-year-old named Jimmy Connors, who made Rosewell look sadder than Buster Keaton. But this was Connors as the old man at the Open of 1991, and that made it into high theater, because he had always been his sport's Sinatra.

For a couple of weeks that September, he made the Open feel like real sports and not just some kind of yuppie fashion show. Even Connors seemed surprised by the force of the passion from the New York crowds, the attention he was getting from the rest of the country, the ratings his matches were producing for the USA cable network.

So he was sitting around in the men's locker room at the National Tennis Center before one of his matches, and he got to talking about what tennis was like when he came along and took over in 1974, what it was like then and what it had become for all the tennis boys and girls since.

"You want to know the difference between me and somebody like [Andre] Agassi?" Connors said. "I had to win to get rich. People say now, 'Well, Jimmy always had an act.' Bullshit. My act was busting my ass to win titles. And I didn't just need titles, I needed major titles. Now these guys show up and they win a few tournaments and they're made for life."

The players know it, not just in tennis but in all the sports. We know it.

We keep settling for the Best Available, too.

Of course, there are glorious and notable exceptions, from Magic Johnson and Larry Bird to Jordan, from Joe Montana to Mark Messier. Winning with them wasn't some kind of passing fancy. They won and made their scores and it only made them want to keep winning. They made winning a career. They did not just want to be rich, they wanted to be champions. Maybe Jordan is the best example of all. He had made his fortune, made ten fortunes, before he ever won a title with the Bulls. But he also knew that he couldn't buy the place in basketball history, in sports history, that he wanted and deserved with sneaker money or Gatorade money. He needed titles, and when he got the first one, it wasn't enough, so he kept winning titles, and came back from baseball to try to win more. He is the greatest athlete this country has ever produced in team sports.

And when Jordan was rewared by the Bulls with a one-year, $25 million contract for the 96–97 season, no one gave a damn. He is the richest and most gifted athlete of them all, but he cares about winning as if he is one of us. When we saw him in the locker room after the Bulls' first title, hugging the NBA's championship trophy and crying like a baby, we knew that Michael Jordan meant it. And we knew something more: That is the way we want our stars to act, that is the way we want sports to look, that is a picture of Jordan we will remember as well as any dunk.

Except that sports, once you take it out of college or high school or the Olympics, hardly ever looks that way. Because most of these guys don't need trophies or titles to get themselves over. In the old days, before free agency and television changed everything, in what was not just another world for Big Sports but another America, the money that players made for winning a World Series or an NFL championship or an NBA title really mattered to them; sometimes the payoff doubled their salaries for the season. There was a night, when the Boston Celtics were playing the seventh game of the NBA finals against the Los Angeles Lakers, back in the years when it seemed the Celtics always ended up playing a seventh game against the Lakers. Bill Russell was the star and Red Auerbach was still the coach, and Auerbach had finally run out of things to say to his team. He paced outside his team's locker room until he knew he had to go in and do something. When he walked into the room, the first player he saw was Frank Ramsay, the team's sixth man.

"Ramsay," Auerbach said, "you give the pregame tonight."

Ramsay, a thoughtful, dignified man from Kentucky, was caught off guard, but finally he nodded to Auerbach.

"Listen up, everybody, Frank's got something he wants to say," Auerbach said.

There was no need for anyone to listen up. Ramsay never said a word. He just walked over to the blackboard on which Auerbach had scribbled some plays. Ramsay erased the plays, then picked up a piece of chalk and wrote the following:

WE WIN—$10,000
WE LOSE—$5,000

He walked back and sat down in front of his locker.

"Best goddam pregame speech I ever saw," Auerbach would tell me more than thirty years later.

The Celtics won the game, by the way.

That was the 1960s. Before the 1970s were out, before Larry Bird came along to turn the Celtics back into champions again, Auerbach saw the money begin to eat away at sports the way termites would. Not destroying it. Just weakening it. Weakening resolve and weakening even teams like the Celtics. Weakening whole leagues. Everything had to keep growing to keep the money moving around. Leagues had to expand. Dynasties still came along, even if they did not last as long as the Celtics' had in the 1950s and '60s. But more and more mediocrity dominated the landscape. Fifteen years after Frank Ramsay's rousing locker-room speech, the Celtics' sixth man was a player named Curtis Rowe, once a college basketball champion at UCLA. The Celtics had become a terrible team, and Rowe was asked what it was like to lose this many games as a pro after winning all the time in college.

"Ain't no Ws and Ls on my paycheck," Curtis Rowe said.

The guy was ahead of his time.

• • •

Would Frank Ramsay and the rest of Red Auerbach's players have burned to win as much if they were averaging a million dollars a year? We all want to think that way, because it is a way of romanticizing the past in sports even more. But there is no way of knowing. If Connors had gotten rich after one U.S. Open, if he had been able to make the kind of score Pete Sampras made after Sampras won the Open as a nineteen-year-old, would Connors's career have gone the same? Would he still have been busting his ass at the age of thirty-nine?

No way of telling.

No one can dispute the level of talent. At the NBA All-Star Game in 1996, the players included Jordan, Scottie Pippen, Hakeem Olajuwon, Shaquille O'Neal, Penny Hardaway, David Robinson, Patrick Ewing, Charles Barkley, Grant Hill, John Stockton, Karl Malone. They're all going to the Hall of Fame. There is probably more young talent in baseball right now than at any other point in the game's history, starting with Barry Bonds and Ken Griffey, Jr., who are among the handful of the most gifted players who have ever played or ever will play.

(The money didn't do that, by the way. I'm almost certain God did.)

And God knows, Big Sports is like Big Everything Else. What is happening in sports isn't different from what is happening in he motion picture industry, where stars such as Jim Carrey command as much as $20 million a picture. Carrey's salary, though, and similar salaries for stars such as Harrison Ford, aren't the problem, any more than Ken Griffey, Jr., making $7 or $8 million for the Seattle Mariners, is the problem in baseball. The problem is the trickle-down effect. You start with Jim Carrey or Harrison Ford way the hell up there, and you work your way down the food chain, and finally discover that someone named Charlie Sheen is now, in the eyes of the people who run the movie business, worth $5 million a picture.

The same Charlie Sheen who is more famous for turning up in Heidi Fleiss's black book than for anything he ever did at the box office.

You know who Sheen is?

Kenny Anderson.

David Cone.

Neil O'Donnell.

He is the on the same Best Available All-Star Team.

Art Modell used his skyrocketing payroll in Cleveland as one of the reasons why he ended up with the debt the size of his own ego. Modell said the Browns' payroll had doubled in the 1990s. Which seemed about right, because the exact same thing was happening at the exact same time in the movie business. By 1995, the average cost of making a movie was $50 million, double what it had been in 1990.

(Fifty million, by the way, is about the size of a payroll for a top team in baseball these days. Entering the 1996 season, the average salary for a player on the Yankees' twenty-five man roster was two million bucks.)

In September 1995, Joe Roth, the chairman of Walt Disney Studios, said this to the *New York Times*:

"We're at a dangerous level right now. It's not just the actors, who time and time again sell tickets, are getting unbelievable amounts of money. It's that actors who haven't proven that they're consistent box-office draws are showing up in the $10 million range."

He sounds just like the general manager of your ballclub. He could be talking about the payroll for the New York Yankees or the Dallas Cowboys or the Seattle SuperSonics or the Vancouver Canucks. Joe Roth overpays stars in the movie business for the same reason that people running sports teams overpay for Anderson and Cone and O'Donnell and all the rest of them:

Because one of them might pay off.

Chapter Six

'ZO AS IN BOZO

Alonzo Mourning plays for the Miami Heat and used to play for the Charlotte Hornets. He was selected to be a member of Dream Team II and represent the United States and the NBA at the Summer Olympics in Atlanta. He was also, after the 1995–96 NBA season, about to become an unrestricted free agent, and before David Falk began discussing a new contract for Mourning, with the Heat or anybody else, Falk had already let it be known that the total package for his client was going to have to be at least $100 million over the rest of his career, starting with a salary of between $13 and $15 million a season.

Mourning was expected to stay with the Heat. Because of NBA rules about what you are allowed to pay a player that already belongs to you, Micky Arison, the Heat owner, was in a position to pay Mourning more than anyone else and still fit him under the team's salary cap. So Mourning wasn't just a free agent at the right time, he was in the right place.

Think of that place as Neil O'Donnell-ville.

And if you are a fan of the Miami Heat, you can just go ahead and start reaching for your checkbook right now.

Arison, who owns the Carnival cruise line—apparently dropping the *e* from his first name overboard in rough seas—is desperate to justify the way he not only paid for Pat Riley but overpaid. Arison was also looking for a new arena for his team, and the best leverage you get with one of those babies is with a winning team that people want to watch.

Riley, who has turned into the NBA's version of Anthony Robbins, is desperate to win another championship to prove that he can reach the top without Magic Johnson passing the ball in to Kareem Abdul-Jabbar. He is not just coach of the Heat, he is team president, and he was the one who traded for Mourning before the 1995–96 NBA season began.

Result?

It turned out that $100 million was a bit low when Mourning reportedly ended up getting $112 million from the Heat for the next seven seasons.

And you know how he prepared himself to be a $112 million ballplayer in Miami and spend the rest of his career there and live happily ever after?

By treating his own fans—the ones who are going to overpay for tickets as soon as Micky Arison overpays Mourning—as if they were Squeegee Boys trying to wash his windshield.

It seems that Mourning did not appreciate the fact that Heat fans, when afforded the privilege of watching the fourth- or fifth-best center in the NBA play, did not turn out in record numbers; in fact, Heat fans did not support the team much better than they had the year before. And sometimes when they did turn out in big numbers, to watch an opponent like the Bulls or the Knicks, Mourning heard more cheers for the other team than he did for himself.

It made him real crabby.

Surely you see the problem here: It's not just the owners who can act like insensitive bastards, even when they're passing around offers that begin at $40 million and head upward through $100 million. It's the fans, too. And it's not just our money they want. We have to be willing to give them a great big hug, win or lose. And we are never supposed to hurt their feelings. It's not enough to make the trip to the Miami Arena, pay the inflated prices, watch Mourning play for a team that did not even get over .500 until there were fewer than twenty games left in the season. Miami Heat fans are also expected to offer Alonzo Mourning—graduate not only of Georgetown but of the basketball wing of the Dale Carnegie Institute—unqualified support, and cheer to a level that satisfies him.

When Heat fans don't do that, they pick up the papers before the Heat are about to embark on a road trip and read this quote from Mourning:

"I'm kind of happy we're getting out of this city and away from these fans. The fans here are so hypocritical, it's ridiculous. It makes me sick."

Next stop, the Board of Tourism, right?

A month before, Mourning had to be escorted off the court at his home arena because he was not only cursing at a fan behind the Heat bench, he motioned for the man to meet him outside after the game. Mourning's team was losing to the Tornoto Raptors, and the fan behind the bench finally shouted, "You hustle like a girl, Alonzo."

At this point, hurt feelings about what the fan was saying suddenly swallowed up Mourning's hurt feelings about losing a basketball game to an expansion team. So he tried to pick a fight with the guy, until Riley told his center to calm the hell down.

The fan was still shouting back, even after Mourning tried to pick the fight.

"I'm a Heat fan, I support you, that's what's sorry about this," the fan said.

Game ended. Mourning still glaring at the guy. Riley had to grab Mourning by the shirt and walk him off the court.

Not long afterward, Dennis Rodman of the Bulls, the RuPaul of the NBA, was suspended for six games without pay and fined $20,000 for head-butting a referee. The headlines were predictable, and correct: "Butthead." Rodman got what he deserved. He's a walking, tattooed threat to the image of the NBA; and to Commissioner David Stern, image is a sacrament. But Mourning is more dangerous and Stern knows it, because when your teams start overpaying people like Mourning, there is a bit of a problem, and it is this: No one has even bought a single ticket to watch $112 million Alonzo Mourning play.

SO WHAT DO WE DO?

Then Mourning turns around and says ticket buyers make him sick, and you have more of a threat to the league's image than Tattoo Boy will ever be. And there ought to be the kind of best-interest-of-the-game provisions in Stern's job, best-interest-of-the-game muscle, that enable him to whack Mourning around the way he does some punk who goes after the ref. In Stern's league, you automatically get a one-game suspension for throwing a punch at another player, whether you land the punch or not. Stern ought to be able to hand out the same when Alonzo Mourning threatens to throw a punch at a fan who is willing to pay enough to sit behind Mourning's bench and watch him lose to the Toronto Raptors.

If Mourning's agent or the Players Association wants to make it a free-speech issue, Stern should be able to tell the agent and the union to kiss his ass.

Because when Alonzo Mourning makes an idiot of himself on the court and in the papers by threatening to throw a punch at one of his own fans—they call him 'Zo, and this is apparently short for Bozo from time to time—he is really threatening to throw a punch at us all. And he should take some kind of fall for that, learn some kind of lesson, so 'Zo Mourning doesn't go around acting like Bozo Mourning ever again.

Because when Mourning talks about his own fans the way he does, when they don't worship him to his satisfaction, he is more of a butthead than Tattoo Boy Rodman could ever be.

Why does Mourning act this way? For the same reason Modell signed his deal with Baltimore before he asked anybody's permission.

Goes back to the dog.

Because he can.

Chapter Seven

A DIS IS STILL A DIS

Athletes have more contempt for authority, authority of any kind, than at any other time in sports history. On the field of play, off the field, it doesn't matter. It seems that every day another incident in the sports pages makes you want to throw the whole newspaper across the room, just because you'll never get the chance to roll the paper up and smack some of these ballplayers across the head with it.

From the time a kid can hit a ball farther, jump higher, throw longer, than the next kid, he or she gets everything she wants. Forget about college and the pros. It starts much earlier than that, in all the sports. Doesn't matter what sport we're talking about. The competition between coaches and agents in tennis for the next Chrissie/Martina/Monica/Steffi is more vicious than a cockfight. The parents of many of these kids have the *charm* of a cockfight. From the earliest possible age, these kids are taught one thing: If they're good enough, they can have anything they want.

Then, down the road, we all get properly horrified when these kids turn mean when anybody says no to them.

Or, God forbid, disrespects them.

Disses them.

In case you missed it over the past couple of years, as disrespecting and dissing have come careening into our language as if on a water slide, being dissed is not just a capital crime on street corners, but in sports as well. One day during the last basketball season, I got a phone call at my home from Anthony Mason, now with the Charlotte Hornets, but still with the Knicks at the time. Over the Christmas holidays that year, I had written a column about Mason, a player who had knocked around basketball's minor leagues and even had to take a job in Turkey one time before finally making it big with the Knicks. The theme of the column was supposed to be a special Christmas for Mason now that he was making real money. But in the course of our interview, he had told me that all his Christmases were special, that even when he was playing in Turkey, he would make it home to Queens for the holidays.

Nice story.

But about six weeks later, Mason started mouthing off about this and that around the Knicks. In a season when he had been given more responsibility—and more time with the ball—than at any other time in his career, I thought he sounded like somewhat of an ingrate. Basketball fans in New York know that Mason is famous for the odd designs he has shaved into the side of his head. (Who was the first guy to do this, by the way? You know, go into the barbershop and say, "I'd like a little off the top, then just go ahead and carve my girlfriend's name right above my ear"?) So I suggested in a column that he should try "Silence Is Golden" next time he went to the barbershop, because his head had gotten big enough to handle the whole phrase.

Mason called up and began a profane tirade that even I, after twenty years in locker rooms and clubhouses, found colorful.

"How could you do me that way?" he said.

"I thought you were out of line."

"You're not understanding me, motherfucker," he said. "I want to know how you could write what you did on Christmas, then turn around and do this?"

"Because I take these things on a case-by-case basis, that's why."

"I'm warning you, don't you ever come near me again."

I said. "Do you want to talk about this, or did you just call me to deliver this message?"

"Deliver the message, you scab motherfucker. Don't you dare come up to my locker. Don't you *dare* get in my face ever again."

And he hung up.

(I never did figure out the "scab" part, but he was on a roll, why break his flow?)

From his point of view, this all made perfect sense. Anything positive that was written, he was entitled to that. The way he was entitled to the $15 million salary the Knicks were paying him. Anything else was against the law, and had to be dealt with quickly and harshly. So I got it in a telephone call at home. NBC's Hannah Storm got it from Albert Belle during the 1995 World Series, when she wouldn't leave the dugout when he ordered her to (more about that one later). Early in the 1996 season, Belle whipped a baseball at a *Sports Illustrated* photographer who wouldn't stop taking his picture when Belle ordered him to do that. The photographer, Tony Tomsic, ended up with a cut hand. Why?

Tomsic, even though he was just doing his job, was saying "no" to Albert Belle.

Completely unacceptable.

It doesn't matter where the "no" comes from. I did it with Mason in a newspaper column, saying, No, you don't get to act like a jerk. Storm did it with Belle: No, I have a right to be in the dugout, I'm not leaving. Then Tony Tomsic of *Sports Illustrated* wouldn't stop making innocuous photographs of Belle doing some stretching exercises, even when Belle yelled at him to stop. A coach or manager can say no by fining someone, or taking away his playing time. A commissioner or league president can do it with a suspension. And the athletes act as if you have walked into their homes with the intention of cleaning them out.

It's never the amount of money, by the way. These guys get fined $10,000 or $20,000 or even $100,000, and they give you the slouch and the sneer as if it's tipping money. There's more where that came from, are you kidding? That's not what makes them want to fight you.

You're trying to steal their manhood.

Except they don't act like men at all, they act like spoiled, willful children. This isn't about right or wrong anymore, or responsibility, or professionalism, or even maturity. When you break the whole thing down, it isn't even about respect. It's about face. The Pose. The way things look. It's a world that has nothing to do with the fans, or even the games. Just the show one player is putting on for another.

And no one ever does quite enough to stop them.

In one way or another, we're all enablers, from the commissioners on down.

Example: NBA playoff game, spring of 1995, Houston Rockets against the Phoenix Suns. Jake O'Donnell is one of the referees calling the game. At this point in O'Donnell's distinguished career, he is twenty-eight years in the league, is the best-known ref in the sport, perhaps the best the league has ever known. It didn't make O'Donnell perfect. Like all refs, he could get as hotheaded as a player sometimes, and use his whistle like a lethal weapon. But over my twenty years covering pro basketball, he had called more big games than anyone else I knew about. And when a series would arrive at Game Seven, you expected to see Jake in the house. Once the game started, you knew he wasn't going to take any crap from a player or coach. Things were never going to get out of hand.

So here he was at the age of fifty-eight, still on top of his game, right there in the teeth of the Rockets vs. Suns. One of the stars of the series was Clyde Drexler, who had been traded to the Rockets from the Trailblazers in midseason, Drexler was going for his first NBA title, after years of falling short in Portland.

It is also worth pointing out that Drexler hated Jake O'Donnell's guts.

Why? Drexler felt O'Donnell went out of his way to give him a hard time. O'Donnell always laughed the charge off, even as he made it clear that the feeling with Drexler was pretty much mutual.

"He got away with cheap-shot stuff his whole career," O'Donnell said to me once. "I know that's not his image. But it was the way he played. Other guys let him get away with that stuff. I didn't. So he used to go around telling everybody that I had it in for him. And it was total bullshit."

Before a game, refs and captains meet at center court; the ceremony is mostly ritual, like umpires meeting with baseball managers at home plate to go over ground rules all of them know. Except there are no ground rules in basketball. But when the meaningless chatter ended on this night, Drexler extended his hand to O'Donnell.

O'Donnell refused to shake it.

During the game, Dan Majerle had a breakaway for the Suns. Drexler chased him and tried to steal the ball. He missed the ball. Replays would show he also missed Majerle. O'Donnell, trailing the play, whistled Drexler for a foul. He would admit later that he blew the call.

That's not the way Drexler saw it.

This was much deeper. First, O'Donnell had disrespected him by not shaking his hand. Now he was clearly screwing with him in the game. Which made Drexler, always so cool on the court, get so hysterical you'd think O'Donnell had pulled a knife on him. He started cursing the ref all over the place, and threw such a fit that O'Donnell had no choice but to eject him from the game.

Blown call or not, Drexler got himself tossed on merit.

It was a playoff game. His ejection might have cost his team a chance at another NBA title, cost him his best shot at his first.

It absolutely did not matter.

Drexler had been shown up, and he was going to show up O'Donnell, because it was clear in his mind that the sonofabitch was out to get him.

You know who got disciplined by the NBA?

Jake O'Donnell.

The cover story was that he wasn't going to be allowed to work any more Rockets games during the playoffs. But it was a lot deeper than that. Jake O'Donnell didn't work another game anywhere. He was through for the year and, as it turned out, through, period. The league was willing to take O'Donnell back for the 1995–96 season. He retired instead, saying he wanted to spend more time with his teenaged son, who was finally living with him again after a long custody battle. Classy to the end, he refused to say that NBA commissioner David Stern, league vice president Rod Thorn—the top cop of the league—or Darrell Garretson, the league's chief of officials (and longtime O'Donnell adversary), had shoved him out the door.

Taking the high road sucks sometimes, but Jake O'Donnell took it.

Somebody had to.

The league took the side of a star player, and there wasn't anything O'Donnell could do about it, so he shut up and went away. And a year later, when Dennis Rodman was head-butting officials and Nick Van Exel of the Lakers was shoving them, and even Magic Johnson was putting his new big belly on a young ref, all of a sudden Stern and Thorn and everybody else around the NBA offices were doing all this hand-wringing about their referees being treated in this shabby manner.

Guess what? They started it.

They started it with their own shabby treatment of Jake O'Donnell, which sent a message so big and clear it was as if they'd hired a skywriter. In so doing, Stern and his lieutenants didn't just screw one ref, they screwed all of them. They didn't care about what was right, that O'Donnell was as good as they'd ever had calling a game, they were just like players.

Stern and the rest of them cared only how things looked. They didn't want Clyde Drexler or anybody else running around suggesting that Jake held grudges, that he didn't call a fair game, that he played favorites. Because that would put a real bad face on things.

In sports, it keeps coming back to face.

When push came to shove—literally and figuratively—the league went with the player. If somebody was going to be thrown over the side in this kind of dispute, it wasn't going to be a basketball star. But a year later, the league wanted to act very tough with players like Rodman and Van Exel and Magic Johnson when all of them though they could use refs as tackling dummies. Only it was a little late for that.

The message had been sent with O'Donnell and Drexler.

No disrespect intended for Commissioner Stern, of course.

SO WHAT DO WE DO?

So maybe it's time to think about rebates in sports. It has reached the point where there should be provisions for punk-outs the way there are for rainouts. If money started coming out of the ticket window instead of going in, maybe that would get the attention of the people who are supposed to be in charge.

Consider the Los Angeles Lakers, spring of 1996. Magic Johnson has made his comeback, there have been nights out of the past when the Lakers again look like one of the best teams in pro basketball, Jack Nicholson is back in the front row at the Great Western Forum, and a trip to the Forum is no longer the trip to the boneyard it had been earlier in what was turning out to be a disappointing season. The Lakers, combining Magic Johnson's impeccable old basketball values with young talents like Nick Van Exel and Cedric Ceballos, were going places.

Oh, they sure were going places.

First, Ceballos. In midseason, he suddenly bolted the team, citing Personal Problems. (read: Hurt Feelings. Even though the team was hot, winning, and winning big sometimes, Ceballos's playing time—and his points—had diminished because of Johnson's return to the team. Ceballos decided he wasn't getting enough respect from Lakers coach Del Harris). Ceballos's Personal Problems turned out to be so deep and so profound that he not only left the team, he left Los Angeles, and was next seen jet skiing someplace in Arizona.

Maybe the choice for him was to take up either water sports or antidepressants.

Ceballos eventually pulled himself together, rejoined the team, and apologized to his teammates. Everything was supposed to be right again with the Lakers. This new era of good feelings lasted until Van Exel got tossed out of a Lakers–Nuggets game in April and became so incensed at referee Ron Garretson that he shoved Garretson onto the scorer's table. Of course, Van Exel—citing the NBA version of the abuse defense—blamed the referee. He even accused Garretson of doing a stuntman's jump onto the scorer's table as the way to get more sympathy for himself.

Rodman had gotten six games for his head butt? Van Exel got seven games without pay and a $25,000 fine on top of that. When you added in his lost salary, the shove had cost Van Exel nearly $200,000.

And he learned absolutely nothing from that, the way he had learned nothing from what happened to Rodman. When Van Exel called a press conference the next day, he apologized to everybody except Ron Garretson. Including his shoe company, Reebok. One of Reebok's ad slogans has players saying, "This is my planet."

Right. And Van Exel was now officially acting like somebody from the goddamned moon.

The most incensed of all the Lakers about Van Exel's behavior was Magic Johnson. Perhaps the most eloquent statement he made in the aftermath of Van Exel–Garretson was made without Johnson uttering a single word. The look of disgust on his face after he stepped between player and ref was there for the world to see.

"I've seen more this season," Magic said, "than in all my other seasons in basketball combined."

In the days after Van Exel's suspension, Johnson talked and talked, sometimes at such great length you wondered if he ever runs out of saliva. But he had been talking since his comeback began about the lack of respect in the NBA, the lack of real leadership, the lack of values. Now, Johnsons's values off the court, in the wild lifestyle to contract the AIDS virus, had seemingly been formulated at Hugh Hefner's mansion. But when it came to playing ball, he had always sounded like the voice of reason.

Four days after Van Exel, Magic Johnson bumped a ref, got suspended for three games, got his big old butt fined $10,000.

People would have been less surprised if he'd gotten caught in the front seat of Hugh Grant's rental car with Divine Brown.

So it turned out that even Magic Johnson was absolutely fabulous at talking all the talk, but wasn't much good at walking the walk, even if it meant just walking away from a referee. So now, with Van Exel already out of the lineup, the Lakers had set some sort of modern—but probably inevitable—record of having two stars out of the lineup at the same time because they had been suspended for the same hotheaded offense. I'm sure this happened with the '27 Yankees all the time. There were probably all sorts of game stories in the old days that began this way:

"Despite the absence of both Babe Ruth and Lou Gehrig again yesterday, the two sluggers currently suspended for bumping umpires, the Bronx Bombers had enough firepower to get past the Washington Senators . . ."

(Johnson, incidentally, originally blamed the ref, same as Van Exel did. I felt this would have been like Hugh Grant trying to blame the rental-car company.)

And you better believe that while Johnson and Van Exel were out of the lineup for behaving like punks, both of them, Lakers fans should have demanded their money back, and the NBA should have made the Lakers pay them. Teams are allowed to throw fans out of arenas and ballparks and stadiums all the time. You're rude or obnoxious or you break the law, you become drunk and disorderly or obscene, you're gone. You slug somebody working for the team, or in the ballpark, you're subject to arrest and prosecution.

If you're someone who has a season ticket, you can lose your tickets.

Forever.

We saw that at Giants Stadium in New Jersey at the end of the 1995 season. There was a late-December game between the Giants and the Chargers. There had been a huge blizzard that week in the New York/New Jersey area, and despite a maintenance crew the size of the Marines that had been brought in by the Giants, there was still a lot of snow and ice underneath the seats at the stadium by the time the game was played on a Saturday afternoon. The Chargers were still fighting for a playoff spot at the time, but the Giants were on their way to finishing 5–11, and as the game—another losing game—wore on, the fans got more and more bored. More and more pissed off.

Drunker and drunker.

Finally, enough of them got stupid.

(Almost as stupid, social scientists might observe, as a veteran ballplayer putting his hands on a game official.)

All over Giants Stadium, in a show that would be witnessed by a national television audience, people began to reach under their seats and throw ice and snow, first at each other, then on the field. At some points there was so much snow and ice in the air, you thought another blizzard had come rolling into the area. It became a disgraceful scene, and a dangerous one. A veteran equipment manager for the Chargers was hit in the head by a piece of ice and dropped to the ground as if he had been shot. By game's end, the artificial turf at Giants Stadium was so littered with snow and ice, it began to look as if it were littered with garbage. Stadium security began to eject people left and right, pulling tickets, taking names.

Finally, one poor slob, a New Jersey guy named Jeffrey Lange, was captured on television and in the newspaper—most prominently on the front page of my paper, the *Daily News*—gleefully throwing a snowball or iceball as if he were Nolan Ryan throwing one of his famous heaters.

We didn't know that day that his name was Jeffrey Lange, of course. In the true spirit of tabloid journalism, we hunted him down like a dog and finally got his name from his ex-wife (this really was a heartwarming story all the way), and Lange was prosecuted for his actions. He was found guilty of improper behavior and fined $500, plus court fees. The Giants wanted some justice.

Fans should be entitled to the same kind of justice when a player acts as if he is the one drunk and disorderly.

Teams say that you break your contract with them when you make a donkey of yourself at a sports event. I say the team breaks its contract with you when its players make donkeys of themselves during a sports event. You tell me how Nick Van Exel of the Los Angeles Lakers was all that different from Jeffrey Lange, ace of the snowball-throwing staff of Giants Stadium. The Giants were embarrassed by fans in their stadium acting like punks. Lakers fans must have felt cheated when they showed up for the first game after the Johnson belly-bump and saw a team on the court that did not include him or Van Exel.

Jerry Buss, the Lakers' owner, didn't commit any crimes, and neither did Jerry West, the team's general manager. Neither did Del Harris, coach. But you know what? This stuff happened on their watch. Their fans got cheated. Their team broke its contract with those fans.

A team can pull your ticket?

Fair enough.

But the team has to pay for your ticket when the situation is reversed. Because you know what? Pushing a ref around is the same thing as pushing us around.

It really is time to start pushing back.

Even if it's one lousy ticket stub at a time.

Or maybe we should bypass the teams and go right to an even higher power in sports these days:

Sneaker companies.

Write a letter the next time someone like Nick Van Exel steps out of line. Or Rodman. Or Shawn Kemp of the Seattle SuperSonics, another very slow study. At the end of the 1995–96 NBA season, in the last game of the regular season, Kemp took a swing at Tom Hammonds of the Denver Nuggets. Even if you don't connect with this kind of punch—Kemp didn't—you get suspended for a game.

The next game for Kemp was the first game of the playoffs. He absolutely didn't care. He couldn't let some nobody push him around.

Dis him.

So what if a SuperSonics team that had won 185 regular-season games the previous three seasons had lost in the first round of the last two years? All that mattered for Kemp was saving face. At all costs.

Now, no self-respecting Sonics fan was going to give up a playoff ticket in protest at Kemp acting like a hothead. But it doesn't mean they should forget that the star of the team put that team at risk.

So the next time it happens, call Kemp's sneaker company, Reebok. Tell them at Reebok that you are sick and tired of Reebok employees like Shawn Kemp acting like louts. Because it can't hurt. Because we all can't keep bitching about these people if we're not willing to make some kind of stand against their loutish behavior. Make the phone call or write a letter and tell them that you wouldn't buy a pair of sneakers endorsed by Shawn Kemp if the sneakers were lined with fur. Or fax them the same message. Here's the number: 617-341-1532. Leave a message for Paul Fireman, the Reebok chairman, if you have to. Take a swing at some of these suits who sign off an idiotic behavior like this, the way Kemp took a swing at Tom Hammonds of the Denver Nuggets. Maybe that will get everybody's attention.

Call Reebok and tell them Kemp and Van Exel have made you a Nike customer.

See how that message plays on Planet Reebok.

Same goes if the player is a Nike client. Fax Phil Knight at Nike at 503-671-6300, and tell him what you think.

If people are willing to start a letter-writing campaign to wipe out some of the garbage we get on television, why can't we do it in sports?

Chapter Eight

TALKING PIGS

The rebate idea doesn't just apply to your favorite teams, by the way. Let me take a brief detour here.

There is a scene in the movie *Animal House* where the actor Kevin Bacon is being initiated into the pretty-boy fraternity by the psycho named Niedermeyer. Bacon is on his hands and knees in his underwear, and Neidermeyer is spanking him with a paddle. And every time Bacon gets smacked again, he grimaces and says, "Thank you, sir, may I have another?"

With sports fans, this is considered mainstream behavior.

Boxing fans, in particular, bend over this way every time some Pay-Per-View outfit airs what passes for a big fight these days. Usually these fights involve Mike Tyson, now that Mr. Tyson has stopped forcing beauty-pageant contestants to have sex with him in hotel rooms. Tyson is the only real attraction in heavyweight boxing since Muhammad Ali retired. He is also an example of how we have lowered our standards in sports, for both stars and champions, even as the price to watch these people keeps going up.

Tyson sells tickets, and sells these Pay-Per-View fights. There is no question that he is a legitimate draw. It shows you how easily we settle. In his own way, he is the heavyweight champion of Best Available.

Ali's huge fame around the world was a result of his personality, both in and out of the ring. He was stripped of his title when he refused induction into the Army during the Vietnam War, and lost three years out of his career, and came out of it all bigger than ever and more popular. Before he was through boxing, he would earn $60 million in purses and there would not be an athlete as famous, all over the world, until Michael Jordan.

Tyson also lost three years from his career, not because he was a conscientious objector, but because of a rape conviction. Before that, he had cut quite a path for himself through public life, grab-assing any woman he could get his hands on, cracking up automobiles, admitting to physically abusing his wife (now ex-wife), the actress Robin Givens.

Ali had floated like a butterfly and stung like a bee. Tyson had tried everything a different way, as the self-proclaimed Baddest Man on the Planet. In Tyson's case, this meant he was a thug with championship belts, the same as Sonny Liston had been, until Ali—then known as Cassius Clay—had beaten his bad ass for the title in Miami Beach. We settled for that. We settle all the time, and now we had done it in boxing because Ali wasn't coming back. Tyson was regarded as the champ after he lost his titles, he was regarded as the champ while he was in an Indiana prison cell, and the Saturday morning he got out of prison, there was so much media attention you wondered why some grifter promoter like Don King didn't sell that as a Pay-Per-View event. I thought the real beauty of the whole thing was that if you didn't know any of the circumstances and saw the penitentiary-faced walk-around surrounding Tyson, if you saw King already pimping for him again, you couldn't really tell whether Iron Mike was on his way into the slam or on his way out.

But he was out, and soon fighting again, and finally on March 16, 1996, he regained one of the heavyweight titles he had lost to Buster Douglas. Tyson fought an amiable British lump named Frank Bruno in Las Vegas and stopped him before the third round was over.

If you watched the fight on Pay-Per-View, it cost you $39.95.

For about eight minutes of work, Tyson was paid $30 million. When you added the $30 million to what Tyson had made in his first two post-slammer fights, he had made $65 million. Two warm-ups against tackling dummies named Peter McNeeley and Busther Mathis, Jr., and then a shot at Bruno's World Boxing Council title, one that Bruno seemed to have won at the Arthur Murray Dance Studios. Sixty-five million in the bank.

Five million more than Ali made in his boxing life.

And the best part of this isn't what you and I paid to watch, and what Tyson made to give Bruno the kind of spanking Kevin Bacon got in *Animal House.*

The best part is that Tyson thinks he is being underpaid here.

Sixty-five million dollars for three fights that lasted about 17 minutes of ring time, which means Tyson was making about $382,000 a minute.

"I'm not being treated fairly," Tyson said in a conference call with boxing writer the week after the Bruno fight.

Forget about the heartwarming movie *Babe,* we've found a real-life talking pig right here.

If this is all so upsetting to the champ, of course, he could always go back to making license plates.

Boxing doesn't piss off everybody the way the other sports do, just because it is hardly ever around. There is no boxing season. There are only a handful of fighters anybody knows. The only fights that seem to matter are the ones that involve Tyson, because this is the class of a no-class sport, and really all the cable companies and promoters and casinos have. He must be making them money, because he can get $30 million for fighting Bruno. He makes money, the cable companies like HBO and Showtime make money, the take in the casinos goes up every time Tyson's action is in town.

This would all be fine, except there isn't any action.

The product stinks.

This is the sporting culture in this country; a boxer like Tyson can make $65 million for getting into the ring with three tackling dummies and no one has any goddamn idea if he can fight. There was a time when people looked at the young Tyson and wondered where he would rank with the great heavyweights in history, and the idea of that now is funnier than Tyson in a mosque.

We still keep paying to watch him.

Thank you, Mike. May I have another?

SO WHAT DO WE DO?

The only way to stop this, the only way to cut into the profits of everybody is making on a sport that should have been abolished long ago, is to stop paying the money. One of these days we are all going to wise up and sit out something like Tyson–Bruno, and then the price will go down. Or the Pay-Per-View business for this sort of execrable product will just dry up and disappear, and the only money you'll have to pay to watch Tyson on television will be your monthly cable bill.

Or if we do insist on paying, maybe we can demand what one New Jersey cable system, Comcast, gave its customers after the Tyson–Bruno fight:

A rebate.

The people at Comcast Cablevision sold the fight with the guarantee that those who paid the full $39.95 would get a five-dollar refund if the thing didn't last three rounds. It didn't. When Bruno went down in the middle of the third round, so did the price of the fight in New Jersey. "We've made it clear we're doing this ungrudgingly," a spokesman for Corncast said at the time. "We're good sports about this. We made the guarantee and now we're happy to make the credits."

They offered the deal in eight Comcast systems, ones that reached about 500,000 homes in central and northern New Jersey. No one from Comcast would say how many subscribers had purchased Tyson vs. Bruno. But those who did would find the refund in their next cable bill.

Finally, a money-back guarantee for sports fans. It was only five bucks, but we have to start somewhere, or we'll just be crawling around on our hands and knees forever.

Other Voices

DAVE CHECKETTS

Dave Checketts was president of the NBA's Utah Jazz, then president of the New York Knicks, and in 1995 assumed the role of president of Madison Square Garden. He still runs the Knicks, and is also the New York Rangers' representative to the National Hockey League's Board of Governors. He is forty-one years old, and one of the brightest people I have met in sports.

You want me to make sports better for everybody, and not just the fans? That's easy, in three words:

No guaranteed contracts.

Period.

I'll guarantee them for injury—basketball-related injuries—and for illness. That's only right, and I have no problem with that. But there has to be a way in sports that if a player isn't cutting it, guess what? He gets fired. He gets fired and it doesn't matter how much time and money he has left on his contract, he gets nothing. Guaranteed contracts are a way of life now in sports, but they are the thing, especially in basketball, that make too many players, way too many, untradable. I'm not saying the owners are always right in sports, because they're not. I'm not saying owners shouldn't take responsibility for some of the mistakes we've made in sports, and the kind of money we pay. But those long-term guaranteed contracts are killing everybody except the players. And they're the biggest reason why ticket prices keep going up.

I've been around professional sports for most of my adult life, and I have to be honest: I'm sick and tired of guys in sports who make a fortune and as soon as they make it don't feel as if they have to work hard anymore. I'm not ignoring the work they've done to get here, the fact that there are only a certain number of people in the world who can play the game at this level. But you know what? It doesn't mean that they should always be set for life, whether they stop producing or not. That's just my opinion. There ought to be a way to say something like this to guys who keep stepping out of line, on or off the court:

One more incident and guess what, you're fired. I'm not just going to threaten to trade you. You're fired. Gone. And I'm going to call around the league and let the other general managers know what a pain you are.

I know I sound a little worked up. But that's the way things should be.

Chapter Nine

AMERICA'S MOST WANTED: SPORTS DIVISION

Now, back to the main event.

We were talking about athletes' contempt for authority. It's bad enough when it happens on the court or on the field. But athletes don't want to be told "no" even when they break the law.

They expect the same kind of preferential treatment from the legal system they get everywhere else. They want that same stroke from judges and juries and grand juries. It is not a great news bulletin that O. J. Simpson's fame as a football and sports television star helped him beat that double-homicide rap. If you don't believe "The Juice" was still basking in the glow that bathes star athletes all the way through their lives, that still has fans lining up to pay for their autographs twenty or thirty years from the last time they played a game, then you come up looking like as dim a bulb as Christopher Darden when he asked O.J. to try on those stupid gloves.

It certainly isn't a news bulletin to sports fans, or media people, or all the people who run Big Sports. Because to some extent, we are all enablers with these people. We have established how much the fans need their sports, and their sports stars. That is why it is no small thing to ask them to stop buying the sneakers, the jerseys, to stop paying for some sullen old drunk ballplayer to sign some old baseball card.

Those of us in the media? No matter how much sniping we do at sports stars when they have it coming, no matter how many times we cuff them around, we still end up making them bigger than they are.

The owners?

We see the stroke from them every day.

They don't just pay, they overpay.

Same with the sneaker companies. Nike has Michael Jordan? Reebok had to have Shaquille O'Neal. The sky was the limit for Shaq coming out of Louisiana State University, before he had ever done anything in the NBA, proved anything, won anything. (Shaq once defended his athletic record, such as it is, this way: "I've won at every level, except college and the pros." Well, there you go. The big guy must have been a regular Bill Russell in high school, and junior high.) So this is the culture and this is the climate and then we all are shocked when some judge or jury behaves like a fan in a team jersey. Cuts star jocks as much slack as we all do. Treats them like Chosen People. A few years ago, a reporter I know was with some ballplayers who decided to leave a spring training game early. So they are all speeding up the Florida Turnpike and they get pulled over by the cops, and the reporter sits there in the car while the ballplayers trade a speeding ticket for a couple of autographed bats and some tickets to future games.

The reporter doesn't think anything of it.

The deal is consummated, the car goes speeding up the Florida Turnpike, the incident is never reported in the reporter's newspapers, or anybody's else's.

Different strokes for different folks.

Teams do it, sportswriters do it, juries do it. Judges do it. Darryl Strawberry pleaded guilty in 1995 to a felony of income-tax evasion, and the only question when Strawberry did it was this: Would he be allowed to do his jail time before the baseball season started? Only, there wasn't any jail time. A judge in White Plains, New York, announced that no purpose would be served by sending Strawberry to jail, and in that moment acted like some Baseball Annie waiting outside the team bus.

Sometimes very famous institutions such as the University of Nebraska are no better.

Lawrence Phillips, a star running back for Nebraska teams that won national championships in January of 1995 and 1996, never had to plead out to a felony charge, the way Strawberry did. Phillips only had to plead no contest to the charge of dragging an ex-girlfriend down three flights of stairs in the process of beating her up. In the end, the only real cost to Phillips was a suspension that effectively cost him six games of his senior season. He was back in time for Nebraska's victory over Florida in the Fiesta Bowl, and he ran down the field enough in that game to be the sixth pick overall in the NFL draft. Somehow it seemed both ironic and quite fitting that the person who drafted Phillips for the Rams was the one female owner in the league, Georgia Frontiere.

In truth, Phillips's crime against Kate McEwen cost him nothing except counseling time, and time spent on Nebraska coach Tom Osborne's bench. At the time, I defended Osborne's decision not to cut Phillips from the team, whatever Osborne's motives. Everybody seemed to assume that Osborne was keeping Phillips around to win another national title, but Nebraska was so loaded that year, it was going to win that title even if Phillips never got off the bench. And at the same time that Phillips had become Public Enemy Number One on the sports page, Warren Moon was still quarterbacking the Minnesota Vikings with a spousal-abuse rap hanging over his head.

(Moon and his wife Felicia had a big fight, in front of their children. It ended with his hands around her neck. Their seven-year-old son was alarmed enough about what he was seeing his father doing to his mother that he was the one who dialed 911. In the aftermath of all this, Felicia Moon didn't want to press charges against her husband. Texas law said it wasn't up to her. On the witness stand, Felicia Moon—looking like a classic battered wife to me—took the blame for just about everything. Warren Moon got off. He was lucky enough to have a wife who clearly believed in special circumstances for people like him. Sometimes in sports, you really do get a lifetime scholarship.)

Phillips had committed a violent, dangerous act against Kate McEwen. But at the same time, Moon was going along without missing a day of work. As it turned out, Felicia Moon had tried to get a restraining order against her husband in the past. As far as anybody knew, this was Lawrence Phillips's first offense. So Osborne didn't cut Phillips loose. Phillips didn't lose this job. he didn't lose his chance to become a No. 1 pick in the draft. He didn't lose his scholarship.

Someone did, though. Nebraska pulled the basketball scholarship of Kate McEwen, Phillips's victim.

Now, the school assured her that she would certainly have her expenses covered for her final year of school. Just no basketball scholarship. Osborne had nearly wept telling us how much that he believed Phillips—the perp—needed the structure of the football program. But his athletic department apparently could not give Kate McEwen the same consideration.

Now we had an entire college administration of talking pigs.

How do you fight the pigs like these? Here is one way: If you are a woman at the University of Nebraska, you call up the National Organization of Women (just because we don't have a National Organization of Sports—yet) and point toward the athletic department at Nebraska, and say, "Get 'em." Believe me, it will get their attention. Even in Lincoln, Nebraska, they won't like picket lines outside the stadium while all the future Lawrence Phillipses inside are trying to win the Cornhuskers yet another national title. They don't want NOW chasing them around, now or ever. You want to know why International Creative Management dropped O.J. as a client after he was acquitted? Whatever the company's stated reasons, I will tell you exactly why: Because ICM (and I'm an ICM client) didn't want NOW and every other women's group in the country on its ass into the next century, that's why.

When Nebraska decided to reinstate Kate McEwen's basketball scholarship a month after they took it away, they weren't necessarily caving in to pressure from women's groups. This time, Nebraska decided it didn't want to have the whole world on its ass for a policy decision they all should have had to scrape off the bottoms of their shoes. They didn't do it to be right, or noble, or out of concern for Kate McEwen. All of them in the Nebraska athletic department were just more people in sports worried about how things looked.

Sometimes the people most worried about face are wearing banker's suits.

But always remember that they did cave in to pressure, from the women who called and wrote the university, from the terrible coverage they got in newspapers and on television and on editorial pages.

The kind of coverage the New England Patriots were about to get when they drafted a career bum out of the Nebraska program, this one named Christian Peter.

Christian Peter is a 6'4", 300-pound defensive tackle who looks as if he majored in smashing beer cans into his forehead and apparently thinks real sports lies not in blocking offensive linemen as big as he is, but in putting women into headlocks.

A few months after helping Nebraska win that second straight national title, Peter pleaded no contest to charges that he grabbed a woman around the neck and harassed her in a Nebraska bar. He was sentenced to ten days in jail and given a $300 fine.

In May of 1994, Peter received 18 months' probation on a charge of third-degree sexual assault on Natalie Kuijvenhoven, a former Miss Nebraska who said he twice grabbed her between the legs and verbally abused her in another Nebraska bar.

Christian Peter has also been named in a federal suit that claims he twice raped a Nebraska coed as far back as 1991. When the woman finally reported the assaults in 1993, her car's tires were slashed, her windshield was broken, and she received death threats on the phone.

It is unlikely that any of this was done by Oklahoma fans.

The woman said that Peter's status as a Nebraska football star kept her from filing charges. Finally, in the summer of 1994, tired of waiting for the school to do something about her charges, she filed a sex-discrimination suit against both Christian Peter and the University of Nebraska. (The rape charges, incidentally, are supported by another young woman in her dorm. This other young woman apparently didn't faint with shock, because *she* says Peter, drunk, had once tried to expose himself to her at some festive Nebraska function. All of this information was available to teams interested in drafting Christian Peter.)

Despite the fact that all these things allegedly kept happening to women who happened to intersect with Christian Peter, a silly old romantic, he was still voted team captain by his teammates by the largest margin in the school's history.

The day after Lawrence Phillips was drafted by the Rams in the first round of the NFL draft, Peter was drafted by the New England

Patriots in the fifth round. By the same Robert Kraft who believes that owning a sports team is the same as being the caretaker of a public trust. On this day, Patriots personnel director Bobby Grier said, "We were well aware of his off-field problems. We did our normal investigation. We know this is a little bit of a controversial pick for us, but Peter understands what this organization stands for, that we're not going to stand for any of those shenanigans off the field or anything that's going to put a bad light on this franchise or the community."

Shenanigans.

Assault and alleged rape.

Just another blip on our radar screen in sports, right?

Bill Parcells said this after the Patriots drafted Christian Peter: "I think once he gets in a good, solid structure, everything will be fine." And of course he was talking about a world, "the sports world," where there is no structure anymore, where athletes with values are more and more viewed as oddballs. Coaches like Parcells talk about structure in sports as if team meetings and tight practice schedules will rehabilitate someone like Christian Peter, as if there is some rehab program for louts like him.

All crap, from Bill Parcells and Tom Osborne and everybody else.

Three days after the Patriots drafted Peter, the heat became so great that the team renounced its draft rights to him. Personnel man Bobby Grier said, "Unfortunately, we did not have complete information regarding Christian Peter's record at the time we made our draft selection." Whether they did or did not became irrelevant. A couple of days after the draft, *Boston Globe* columnist Eileen McNamara had gone after Peter and the Patriots as if she were the star defensive tackle rushing the quarterback. She cited chapter and verse on the amazing list of charges against Peter, which also included an alleged threat to kill some parking attendant back in Nebraska, and urinating in public. At this point, Myra Kraft, wife of

Bob Kraft, had gone to her husband and said she didn't think the Patriots should be in the business of hiring sex offenders, and told her husband to get rid of Christian Peter.

Which he certainly did.

Sometimes you don't need the National Organization of Women to get action in sports.

Sometimes you need only one woman.

Christian Peter, national champion football star, in his own words (a taped interview with ESPN, after the 1996 NFL draft):

"I have nothing to hide. I've been accused of some major allegations. All are lies. Uh, I've owned up to some minor mistakes I've made. I've said, ya know, that I have used some poor judgment in some situations. But the major allegations that have been made against me are total lies. Uh, ya know, there's three allegations about how I've assaulted women. They're lies. I have a mother and a sister and I know that if someone did something like that to them, I could never forgive them. But this isn't the situation. I have never assaulted a woman. And I would never do something like this.

"The one who claimed I raped her, there was no rape, this was two adults having consensual sex. She didn't come out until two years later, and it was looked into by the city police and the campus police and they found there was nothing there. This is a girl who said she felt threatened. That's ridiculous. Here's a girl who continually called me. Had other players come up to me and said why isn't Christian [calling me]? This is a girl who worked in the football office and had opportunities to talk to Coach Osborne and never showed up. This is a girl who flat-out lied about what happened between me and her."

Question: "What motive would she have to lie?"

Peter: "Ya know, I don't know. She comes out five years later and there was no criminal charges and so she files a civil suit right before I'm about to go into the NFL draft and come across some money. Anyone with a decent head on their shoulders can see what's going on. Uh, it's just not the truth. The thing that I think keeps going through all this is that I know the truth about all these situations. I know what Christian Peter is and my family knows who I am. The people close to me, my coaches, my teammates, know what I'm about, and how I've been portrayed in the media, all the negative publicity I've received that's not fair. Uh, these girls say they're the victim. The victim is Christian Peter. I'm the one who's suffering."

Question: "Why would you plead no contest to something that never happened?"

Peter: "It never did happen. Uh, this was the advice I received from the lawyer who said it was the best thing to do at the time. No, I didn't grab this female in a bar. Uh, she never identified me. I was identified by a former football player who I came in with who was later kicked off the team because he was a slacker, he wasn't a hard worker, he brought the team down, he had no business being on the Nebraska football team, and I believe out of revenge he was the one who identified me. No, I did not assault this girl in a bar. Uh, I took the blame for someone who did, for someone close to me and, uh, at the time it was the right thing to do. His penalty would have been a lot harsher than my penalty was."

Question: "Alcohol seems to be involved in a great many of these incidents, doesn't it?"

Peter: "Christian Peter is not an alcoholic. Yes, I do have a drinking problem. Yes, I do seem to use poor judgment when I drink. Uh, it's something that's being corrected. I no longer drink."

Question: "Let me just read this [psychological profile] to you, and I want you to tell me whether or not this is accurate: 'Christian Peter is an individual who either lacks intelligence, or maturity, or tends to be selfish. He may be a combination of all those traits.'"

Peter: "You know, I don't think I'm a risk to anyone. Like I said, I've owned up to minor mistakes I've made. I will not own up to the major accusations that have been made about Christian Peter, because they are lies."

Question: "Is there anything you would like to tell the National Football League?"

Peter: "Christian Peter is the victim. I'm not Attila the Hun. I'm not some barbarian that runs around going crazy. . . . To know me is to love me."

He hasn't learned anything. And that's really not the scary part. The scary part is that neither had the Patriots before they drafted him.

Chapter Ten

ENEMIES LIST

Oh, and there's lots more. You remember this one, don't you?

On the night before his thirtieth birthday, Michael Irvin decided to throw himself a party. Not at his opulent home in the Dallas suburbs, with his wife and two children. Irvin, the Cowboy wide receiver who is one of the best players of his time in pro football—on one of the best teams of all time, the Cowboys of the 1990s—instead chose a Residence Inn not far from Texas Stadium, where the Cowboys play their home games. The guest list for Irvin's party was as small as its setting: Irvin, two topless dancers, an ex-teammate. The party favors were as follows:

Two ounces of cocaine.
Three ounces of marijuana.
Enough drug paraphernalia for the four of them to build a model car.

It is worth pointing out here that Irvin is not just one of the most famous professional athletes in America, he also plays for as famous a team as we have right now. The Cowboys of the '90s are as much of an attraction as Michael Jordan's Bulls, more of an attraction than Shaquille O'Neal's Orlando Magic, or a Cleveland Indians baseball team loaded with sluggers and able to sell out an entire season, all eighty-one home dates, before it even begins. Through January of 1996, they had won three of the last four Super Bowls. Nobody had ever won three in four years before. No other team had a flamboyant, hey-look-at-me owner on the sidelines like Jerry Jones. No other team had four stars like these: quarterback Troy Aikman, running back Emmitt Smith, cornerback/wide receiver/kick returner Deion Sanders.

And Michael Irvin.

Before the 1995–96 season, Irvin has signed a new $15 million contract with the Cowboys. He had his own radio show in Dallas, his own television show, he appeared in television commercials. One of seventeen children, he had grown up in part of Fort Lauderdale, Florida, never shown in brochures distributed by the Chamber of Commerce. Irvin was known for his extraordinary toughness on the football field, his ability to shove a defender away from him and then outleap everybody for the ball. Off the field, he had shoved aside a disadvantaged childhood and reached for the sky. He should have been the poster boy for all the other dreamer kids in all the places like the section of Lauderdale in which he had grown up. He had shown them that a background like his didn't have to be a death sentence.

Irvin had made it. He was about to turn thirty, and he had all the money and fame and worship to which the modern American athlete is supposed to aspire. Sure, he could still act like a punk, the same as he had when he had been a rowdy kid at the University of Miami, the home office for rowdy kids in college football. There was the moment after the Cowboys had beaten the Packers in the NFC championship game when Irvin shouted the word "shit" into a live mike, so that not only Texas Stadium but a national television audience could hear him loud and clear.

Cowboys fans forgave him immediately. They wanted to win another Super Bowl, and they weren't going to win one without Michael Irvin catching passes from Aikman. They would do what fans generally do when one of their heroes misbehaves, and look the other way. Or blame it on the microphone: If people don't want to hear that sort of language right after the game, don't put the mike in front of someone like Mike.

Fans spend as much time looking the other way in sports as they do looking at the games.

But now, on the night before his birthday, the night before he was scheduled to play husband and daddy at home with his family, Irvin was willing to blow everything—literally and figuratively—for one night of big fun in a motel room.

Irvin? He was about to become a different kind of poster boy, to represent all the rich young athletes like him who have no respect for who they are, where they are, where they have come from, how lucky they are to lead the kind of lives Big Sports has enabled them to lead. Instead, they treat their own success with contempt. If they are loyal to anything, it is to their own sense of entitlement, not just for the money and the fame, but for perks like the ones Irvin had found in the Residence Inn.

These are the young athletes who make us want to blow a hole in the television set every time *SportsCenter* on ESPN leads another nightly sportscast with another story like this.

Here was Michael Irvin, another real-life talking pig from sports. He had heard the cheers in the NFL's stadiums; he had this extraordinary stage every Sunday, not just in the stadiums, but in front of all the millions watching pro football on television. And no team anywhere got ratings the way Irvin's Cowboys did.

Now the stadium was a motel room, with cops coming through the door.

Irvin knew all about trouble with cops before this. He had been accused by a woman—not Mrs. Irvin—of assault in a nightclub parking lot. He was once cited for disorderly conduct after an incident at a Florida convenience store. Along with several of his Cowboys teammates, he was charged with taking tickets from an airlines agent who was later accused of stealing the tickets. The tickets were probably just more goodies to which Irvin thought he was entitled.

Only this time Irvin had graduated to real trouble, trouble that would finally end with Irvin pleading no contest to a felony change of drug possession, and more hours of community services than he probably ever spent inside a classroom at the University of Miami.

At the time, some people said, Well, look on the bright side.

At least he had graduated from something.

More crime news to cheer everybody up:

According to a story in the *Los Angeles Times* at the end of 1995, there were 252 criminal incidents of one kind or another, involving 345 athletes and team personnel, reported nationally between January 1 and December 15 of that year.

By then it had reached the point where you really did think we needed a crime docket of some kind on the "Transactions" page that most sports sections have now for standings and box scores and trades and the like. That way, they could cover complaints against athletes, formal charges, arrests, convictions, without taking space away from stories about our heroes.

The breakdown in the *Los Angeles Times* went like this:

Total college	209
Total professional	136
College football	160
Pro football	49
College basketball	35

Baseball	25
Pro basketball	21
Hockey	21
Boxing	18
Others	16

According to the *Times* story, athletes were convicted 68 percent of the time, about the same as the general population. But in cases involving domestic violence, athletes were convicted only 36 percent of the time, less than half the rate of the general population. Why the lower conviction rate? First of all, athletes are more frequently arrested on sexual assault charges—even if to know them is to love them—and that increases the pool of cases. Second? You started to hear it from Christian Peter, and you hear it all the time from athletes:

She knew who I was.

She wanted it.

She wasn't the one who said no to me, it was the other way around. Now she's trying to get at my money.

The bitch.

Why are there so many crimes by athletes against women? Because, from a very early age, women are just viewed as being goodies, along with shoes and clothes and cars. Perks of the job. To be discarded like the shoes the athletes endorse when the next woman comes along. When they grow up in a culture where the answer is supposed to be yes, "no" comes out like something in a foreign language. It's almost as if young jocks in this country are hearing something from sports that is like rap music. People worry all the time in sports about performance-enhancing drugs such as steroids; they want to blame a lot of athlete crime on what is known as the "'roid rage." But how can even steroids be more intoxicating than the fame and the money and the power that comes with them?

And you bet your ass that power like that corrupts absolutely in sports, the way it does anywhere else. Maybe more. It is always worth remembering that we are infrequently dealing with Fulbright scholars here. So the stories keep coming and we keep finding out about athletes, college and pro, and sometimes all the way back to high school, acting in a manner, without remorse, that scares the hell out of you. A recent study conducted by the University of Massachusetts covered thirty colleges, and here is what they found out: Male athletes were involved in 19 percent of campus crimes, even though they only made up 3.3 percent of the campus population.

So it's not just crime against sports we get, and crimes that we feel have been committed against us. It's crime, period. There was a day early in 1995, January 28 to be exact, when most of the front page of the sports section in the *Los Angeles Times* was devoted to crime-related stories. Darryl Strawberry was plea bargaining on his tax charges. A story about Art Schlichter, the gambling-addicted ex-Ohio State football star, and his problems with bank fraud. Another story about a Chargers wide receiver whose brother was on death row in Florida.

Just another fun-filled day in the world of fun and games.

No wonder sports fans wake up whistling all the time.

Three months of sports crime, January through April of 1996.

A partial list:

JAN. 2: Kenny Walker, once a No. 1 draft choice of the New York Knicks, a former Kentucky basketball star, is arrested in Lexington, Kentucky. Police charge him with the choking of his wife, Rosalind.

On the same day, ex–Georgetown star Sleepy Floyd, who went on to a long career in the NBA, is arrested after a fight with his wife.

Neither basketball star mentions if he is the real victim.

JAN. 5: Albert Belle is sued by the guardian of the teenager accused of throwing eggs at Belle's house the previous Halloween. The sixteen-year-old boy contends that Belle chased him in his Ford Explorer and bumped him with the car after the egging.

Belle is charged with reckless operation of a motor vehicle and fined $100.

They should have charged him with reckless operation of a reckless life.

JAN 8: Tennis star Steffi Graf's father Peter refuses to testify before a panel investigating the allegations that he and some German officials weren't being paid on his daughter's income. Peter Graf had been arrested the previous August on charges that he failed to pay taxes on $35 million of Steffi's income over a period of years.

Sometimes you don't even have to be a sports star to believe you live outside the world of rules.

Sometimes you just have to be related.

JAN. 9: Rickey Henderson, baseball's all-time stolen base leader, now with the San Diego Padres, is reported to be under investigation by the Internal Revenue Service for possible unreported income from baseball card shows.

These stories, of course, have become more common than ones about athletes wanting to renegotiate their contracts. Card and memorabilia shows, with current stars and ex-stars, have become the Times Square of Big Sports, with about the same level of charm.

There is more warmth between hookers and johns than there is between the signers and their devoted fans.

JAN. 14: Tony Dumas of the Dallas Mavericks is arrested in the early morning for filing a false auto-theft report after fleeing the scene of an accident. The police say Dumas fled the scene three hours before he filed the report, saying his car had been stolen at gunpoint.

After being arrested, Dumas said, "It was just a fender bender and no one was hurt."

So why not lie to the police?

JAN. 15: Albert Belle now admits to knocking down the vicious sixteen-year-old Halloween vandal.

"As soon as I caught up with him, I slammed on the brakes and was jumping out of the car and was going to run after him," Belle told the *Morning Journal* of Lorain, Ohio. "It was raining and it was kind of mucky back there."

Perhaps Belle thought that in a competition between a Ford Explorer and a kid on foot, wet conditions make the whole thing into much more of a fair fight.

JAN 16: Cincinnati Bengals defensive lineman Dan Wilkinson, the No. 1 overall pick in the 1994 NFL draft, is found guilty of striking his pregnant girlfriend during an argument the previous September. Wilkinson pleads no contest—the jock's best friend—and is given a six-month suspended sentence by Judge Dennis Helmick in Hamilton County Municipal Court. He could have been jailed for up to six months on these charges.

At least in Helmick's court, Big Dan Wilkinson was still number one, even after cuffing around a pregnant woman.

She was probably just another woman around another famous athlete asking for it, right?

On the same date Herve Filion, the winningest driver in the history of harness racing, is arraigned in White Plains, New York, on criminal charges stemming from allegations that he and three other drivers fixed races at Yonkers Raceway. The indictment charged Filion and three others with grand larceny and conspiracy in the theft of more than $200,000 in losing bets on races they allegedly fixed.

JAN. 26: Buffalo Bills receiver Russell Copeland is scheduled to appear in Hamburg, New York, Town Court on charges that he broke his girlfriend's nose in a fight. Natasha Cook, twenty-three, told police she and Copeland had been arguing when he threw a phone against the wall and hit her with it.

(Hey, the guy's a receiver, not a quarterback.)

On the same date, Giants quarterback coach Steve DeBerg is arrested in the early morning and charged with drunken driving after going the wrong way down a one-way street in Manhattan. DeBerg refuses to take a Breathalyzer test and has his license revoked on the spot.

JAN. 29: Lavonnie Wooten is convicted in Phoenix of murdering twenty-seven-year-old Althea Hayes, the pregnant girlfriend of his cousin, former Suns forward Jerrod Mustaf. An aspiring singer, Hayes was three months pregnant by Mustaf when she was shot in the head in her suburban Glendale apartment in 1993. During the two-week trial, *both* the prosecution and defense argued that Mustaf had ordered the killing because Hayes refused to have an abortion. Due to lack of evidence, Mustaf was never charged. Glendale police continue to investigate.

Mustaf went off to play ball overseas.

JAN. 30: Darryl Strawberry, who sometimes can feel like a one-man crime blotter, pleads not guilty to charges that he ignored a court's order to make child-support payments for his two children from a previous marriage. His former wife, Lisa, contends that Strawberry—reported to be nearly broke in the same decade in which he signed a $20 million contract with the Dodgers—owes her more than $370,000 in payments.

FEB. 6: Anthony Tucker, a reserve forward with the New York Knicks, is arrested at 4:24 A.M. on charges of assaulting two New York City police officers, resisting arrest, and driving while intoxicated. The 6'8" Tucker reportedly punched one officer in the face after being pulled over in Manhattan for blocking traffic.

And you know what I bet happened?

Those police officers probably dissed him, too.

Anthony Tucker, whoever he is, couldn't stand for crap like that.

FEB. 11: Chargers defensive end Shawn Lee is arrested outside a New York City nightclub and charged with assault and resisting arrest. Lee, who weighs in at about three hundred pounds, is accused of throwing another nightclub patron against a wall, gashing the man's head.

FEB. 13: Jury selection begins in the spouse-abuse trial of Warren Moon. This is the one about Moon being charged with a Class A misdemeanor for choking, striking, and scratching his wife Felicia.

FEB. 22: Villanova basketball star Kerry Kittles is suspended from his team's last three regular-season games by the NCAA. The charge? Unauthorized use of one of the university's telephone charge cards.

"I'm totally embarrassed for letting down Villanova University," Kittles says.

And getting caught.

FEB. 28: Belle, the poster child for everything we love about Big Sports in the '90s, is fined $50,000 for his dugout tirade against NBC's Hannah Storm before the third game of the 1995 World Series. It is the third-largest fine in baseball history, eclipsed only by the fines Lonnie Smith and Dave Parker paid in 1986 in connection with cocaine cases.

Here is what happened that night in the Series, by the way: Belle came out for batting practice and found the Indians' dugout filled with loathsome media scum. He began a profanity-laced tirade aimed at everybody, and cleared the dugout. Except for Ms. Storm, who was waiting with her crew because she had an appointment with Belle's teammate, Kenny Lofton.

"I'm talking to you, you asshole!" Belle yelled at Storm.

"Get the fuck out!" he yelled.

This went on against Hannah Storm for five minutes.

Another tough guy with a woman.

Belle just didn't leave any marks.

MARCH 4: Michael Irvin is arrested in Texas with the self-employed models and the $6000 worth of cocaine.

MARCH 4: Christian Peter is cited for his third-degree assault. It is his eighth arrest since September of 1991. This one is for the headlock on the woman in Kearney, Nebraska.

Probably wanted it.

Don't they all?

MARCH 15: In an odd but festive St. Patrick's Day celebration, former Los Angeles Dodgers outfielder Willie Davis is arrested while waving a samurai sword in an argument with his parents. Davis wanted money and threatened to kill them if they didn't comply.

MARCH 19: Former NFL running back Sammie Smith pleads guilty to two federal charges of possession and distribution of cocaine and faces a minimum of twenty years in prison. Smith, twenty-nine, is accused of being one of central Florida's major suppliers of crack cocaine to the Orlando-area communities of Zellwood and Apopka, where he grew up.

Local boy makes good.

MARCH 26: A grand jury in Rockwall, Texas, indicts Steelers running back Bam Morris after authorities reported finding marijuana and cocaine in his car. Morris was the top rusher in the Super Bowl game between the Steelers and the Cowboys played just two months before.

This is perhaps the first time in pro football history that two stars of the same Super Bowl game have drug raps against them in the same state at the same time.

Some fans in Pittsburgh and Dallas are pretty outraged about that.

They also wonder if their heroes will be ready to open the season.

Especially in Dallas, where fans are used to Cowboys breaking the law. It is practically a tradition down there, like the Texas–Oklahoma game in college football. In the months leading up to the Cowboys' third Super Bowl in four years, defensive back Clayton Holmes and defensive lineman Leon Lett were both suspended because of drugs, Holmes for cocaine, Lett for marijuana. Erik Williams, a star for the team in the offensive line, nearly killed himself after slamming his Mercedes into a wall following a team party. Williams pleaded no contest—in sports, never go away from a winning hand—to drunk driving. Not long after that, Williams was charged with sexually assaulting a seventeen-year-old topless dancer.

Those charges got dropped. Williams settled with her out of court.

On and on it goes. In the aftermath of Irvin's arrest, it was also discovered that several members of the Cowboys were renting a party house known to them as the "White House." The house was located in a suburb not far from Valley Ranch, where the team practices. According to people who lived in the neighborhood, Cowboys players were seen coming out of the house at all times of the day and night, usually with women who were not wives or girlfriends.

According to stories, wives or regular girlfriends weren't allowed at the White House. That was a rule.

And I keep saying there aren't any rules in sports.

While all this is going on, Cowboys owner Jerry Jones signs a linebacker named Broderick Thomas. You want to know who this firecracker is? He's somebody who got fined by the Minnesota Vikings because he had been arrested twice in the same year, once for carrying a weapon and the other time for drunk driving.

A born Cowboy.

As long as people like Jones continue to sign people like Thomas, as long as the New England Patriots continue to draft people like Christian Peter, then nothing is going to change in sports. And the people doing the drafting and the signing and looking the other way about what goes on in the bars and after the bars and in seedy places like the White House are going to come across as being dumber than self-employed models.

The next time you go mad cheering Michael Irvin, so are you.

And why should current athletes have all the fun?

Here is something for the alumni association: On May 3, 1996, former New York Giant Lawrence Taylor, one of the true immortals in pro football history, perhaps the greatest defensive player the game has ever known, is arrested for trying to buy $100 worth of crack cocaine from an undercover agent in Myrtle Beach, South Carolina.

No one who had followed Taylor's career on and off the field was even remotely surprised to hear about this. He had tested positive for drugs twice in his career, been suspended once, which put him one positive test away from a lifetime suspension. There had been times during his career when he even bragged about cheating on his league-administered drug tests. And when he finally did end up in rehab, he fled after a couple of days. When he wrote an autobiography, he sneered at the other addicts in the room with him, said he felt uncomfortable being around all those "crazies."

They were in rehab trying to get well and he was trying to blow a million-dollar career and one of the most remarkable talents for football God had ever given anybody, and they were the ones who were crazy.

The guy was a sight to behold sacking the quarterback, but from the time he showed up at Giants Stadium out of the University of North Carolina, one thing was quite clear. You could park cars inside Lawrence Taylor's head.

He said he didn't need rehab because golf had cured his addictions. I thought he should open a chain of LT Pitch-and-Putt Rehab Clinics. If you could putt the ball through the windmill on number 18, you could not only win a free round, you could pronounce yourself cured of drug addiction. Only two years into his retirement, golf didn't seem to be doing the trick anymore for Taylor. Because when he was picked up for trying to buy the crack—it wasn't real crack, but Taylor didn't know that when he swallowed it, at least smart enough to know he had been pinched—Taylor was in South Carolina to play in a celebrity golf tournament.

Now for anybody living anything close to a normal life, something a million miles from the life of a modern celebrity sports star, an arrest like that, in circumstances like these, would be a life-shattering experience.

Here is how Taylor handled it:

First, he reached into his pocket and paid his $5000 surety bond in cash.

Then he gave an interview to a local newspaperman and asked the following question:

"Is this going to be in the newspaper?"

Not "I'm sorry."

Not "I really screwed up this time."

Or "I need help."

"Is it going to be in the newspaper?"

He wasn't as worried about what he had done as he was about how it looked. About face. It always comes back there for the rappers of sport. He wasn't worried about what the story was, he was worried about its play. He wasn't as concerned about some cheap crack buy from a stranger as he was that he had gotten caught. And coming from where he comes from, having been one of the most celebrated football players who ever lived, on one of the most well known teams in sports history, it was entirely predictable.

You don't even have to be as big a star as Taylor was to think this way, by the way. I am always reminded of the time in 1994 when linebacker Winston Moss of the Raiders punched Rick Mirer, the Seattle quarterback that day, after tackling him. Just hauled off and gave him a good shot. The refs didn't see it, as it turned out. A huge brawl ensued. After the game, Winston Moss had this to say to reporters:

"It's not a cheap shot unless you get caught."

So Taylor had been caught. But he had the money to post his bond. Pulled himself together and gave an interview. It was the usual whine we get when an athlete gets caught. No one understood what he'd been going through. There were mean headlines back in New York about him being late with child-support payments (hey, there's so much golf, so much dope, so little time), headlines calling him, the great LT, old Number 56, a deadbeat dad.

He said he was even thinking of killing himself.

That's always a last resort for the Jock in Trouble. Darryl Strawberry tried it in the *New York Post* right before he pleaded guilty to the tax-dodge felony. After lifetimes of getting everything else on demand, they want sympathy, too. And, by God, if they don't get it, they will stick their head in the oven.

So that was Taylor's very busy day around eighteen holes of celebrity golf. But he wasn't through yet. After the golf and the bust and eating the fake dope and posting bond and giving his interview and threatening suicide, you know what Taylor did next?

He went to an autograph signing.

The lines were longer than ever.

The pay, of course, was real good.

SO WHAT DO WE— DO?: I

These are our sports heroes, like it or not.

Not all of them are like this. Not even the majority of sports stars.

Just way too many, and way too often.

Marge Schott talking about "million-dollar niggers" will always be more dangerous to sports than a coffee table full of dope belonging to Michael Irvin or somebody else. We routinely dismiss all drunk-driving arrests in sports, relegate them to corners of the newspaper and sportscasts reserved for minor news, even though a drunk ballplayer behind the wheel of a car is more a threat to sports fans on the road with him than some ballplayer with a couple of joints in his pocket.

But more and more, as punks like Irvin get slaps on the wrist from judges and commissioners and team owners, you want there to be some kind of official Sports Police to handle these cases properly, to give all the Irvins of the world some sort of punishment that will:

(a) Satisfy the fans who help pay Irvin's salary and make him the kind of celebrity he is.

(b) Teach him a goddamn lesson.

Believe me, one of these days the people who run sports are going to figure out how important (b) really is. One of these days, there is going to be punishment to fit crimes, not just against the drug laws, but against sports. Unions in sports are always screaming about the players' rights in cases like these. Bully for them. But what about ours? The unions should understand something sports fans understood long ago, as the crime docket kept getting longer and longer on the sports page: Every time someone like Irvin makes this kind of spectacle of himself, he damages others in the union the way he damages everything else.

There should be sports laws about athletes who break real laws, and they should have some teeth in them. Don't let someone like Irvin think he can get himself out of trouble and over it by doing twenty-eight days in some rehab clinic and then coming out and crying to *Sports Illustrated* or *People* magazine or even Barbara Walters about how sorry he is.

It shouldn't be that easy for them to get over.

Put clauses in these zillion-dollar contracts about law-abiding behavior, and if the unions and agents and ballplayers themselves don't like the clauses, tell them all to go find another sport or another league that will pay $15 million, or $50 million, or $100 million for athletes who think it's cute to act like juvenile delinquents as they're about to turn thirty.

Bigger the crime, bigger the penalty.

The more you make, the more you pay.

You get convicted of a felony, and you are making $4 million a season, you give back half a million to your team, and the team turns it over to charity.

Make it 10 percent of the salary, make it 20 percent, but make it something that hurts. It seems that every couple of days another famous athlete is accused of cuffing around his wife, or his girlfriend, or some woman he met in a bar. You get convicted of that, you lose the same kind of money a drug conviction costs you. Or it costs you half a season.

Without pay.

You lose games in the National Football League for testing positive for steroids, and good for the league in doing that. But again: Who is more of a threat to the whole idea of the league? A thick-necked lineman with steroids in him, or some quarterback trying to beat his wife silly?

Or Michael Irvin?

Michael Irvin had always loved the spotlight. Then the cops came through the door of Room 624 at the Residence Inn and he was caught in a different kind of spotlight. And as he was about to be handcuffed, here is what Irvin—athlete of the '90s—said to those cops in the motel room:

"Can I tell you who I am?"

One of the cops gave him a bored look, and said, "I know who you are."

The cop at least had some respect for his job. This is what he should have said to Irvin:

"Yeah, I know exactly who you are. An asshole."

Irvin was eventually suspended for the first five games of the 1996 season. Without pay. So the bill for Room 624 was really about $500,000 in salary.

You know what?

It still wasn't enough.

SO WHAT DO WE DO?: II

Nothing will ever change as long as we continue to genuflect in front of these guys. Because every time we go down in front of someone like Lawrence Taylor, or buy a book with Dennis Rodman's name on it—not to mention his bare ass—every time a parent thinks it is cute to color a kid's hair the way Rodman does, and so says it is all right to emulate Rodman; every time we sign off on this kind of bullshit and let these people off the hook, saying they are weak or colorful or different or misunderstood, then we forfeit the right to be mad as hell, and sports gets away from us a little more.

I said before that the success and the play received by someone like the late Charlie Finley helped create the monster that is George Steinbrenner.

And if we don't create the Rodman monster or the Michael Irvin monster or the Lawrence Taylor monster, we never do a hell of a lot to stop them, either.

Every time a sports fan stands in a long line and finally pays money for the right to have someone like Taylor sign his autograph—a ritual that is supposed to have something to do with the romance of sports and is more like quick, anonymous sex—that fan is signing off on so much of what we all think is wrong with sports.

But they—we—keep signing off.

Summit, New Jersey, February 1996:

Outside the Garden State Convention Center, there are hundreds and hundreds of fans lined up on a bitterly cold day in the middle of a bitterly cold New Jersey winter. The fans do not complain. They just wait for the doors to open because they know that inside the Garden State Convention Center are their heroes.

In this case, the heroes are the world champion Dallas Cowboys.

While the fans stand in the cold, wanting to be the first inside, the first in line to get a crack at the Cowboys, the ballplayers who have already been paid to show up for this signing are across the street in the warmth of their hotel rooms. But soon they will be paid between $20 (backup quarterback Jason Garrett) and $120 (Troy Aikman) to sign what are described at these shabby functions as Large Items. That means a football or a helmet.

Emmitt Smith signs for $80.

Michael Irvin, not yet caught with the self-employed models or the dope at the Residence Inn, signs for $60.

These functions go on all the time, all over the country, weekend after weekend. Sometimes a promoter hits the jackpot and gets the Cowboys. Sometimes it is retired ballplayers. Always the scene is sad. Sometimes the promoter is a cheap, convicted hustler named Michael (Fat Mikey) Bertolini, who a couple of months before had been sentenced to fourteen months in prison after pleading guilty to a tax-fraud conspiracy stemming from a 1989 autograph show down the New Jersey Turnpike in Atlantic City. At that show, Fat Mikey Bertolini, a bottom-feeder of sports if there ever was one, got together with baseball immortals like Duke Snider and Willie McCovey and decided to keep their profits out of the reach of the government. The government considers this bad form. Bertolini had spent his life majoring in bad form. Now he'd started something that would take him down real good, and take down two of the most famous names in baseball history with him. No moral alarm went off for either Snider or McCovey, and years later they would be humiliated themselves with felony convictions because it did not. It cost them their good names, and it cost them civil penalties.

In court papers, Fat Mikey Bertolini said he gave cash to the Hall of Famers "with the understanding that it wouldn't be reported."

By now, everybody knows about Duke Snider and Willie McCovey and what happened to Darryl Strawberry and how Pete Rose, an old friend of Bertolini's, ended up in jail because of income from card shows and memorabilia that he neglected to tell the government about. The Cowboys know, their agents know. Of course they know. Of course they know with whom they are dealing when they deal with Bertolini (the famous agents of sports would never want to be compared to Bertolini, but they're all in the same club, Bertolini is just lower down the food chain). The Cowboys show up for the easy money anyway.

They show up for Fat Mikey, who helped take down Pete Rose.

Fat Mikey, who was also convicted of assaulting his Atlantic City show partner, another beauty named William Hongach.

(In December of 1995, Bertolini said in court that his career as a dealer in memorabilia began in 1980, when he was just fifteen. Back then, he would just wait for players outside the ballpark, get their autographs, go off and sell them. By the middle of the 1980s, baseball commissioner Bart Giamatti concluded that Bertolini had graduated into being Pete Rose's bookmaker. Destiny brought them together.)

It is all a beautiful thing. An ESPN crew is there to get comments from the players. It is removed from the convention center by a Bertolini flunky, as redundant as that concept is. Larry Brown, the Most Valuable Player of the Super Bowl, drives across the street rather than have to face a single television camera. Emmitt Smith has a single comment to make:

"Get out of my way."

Irvin has nothing to say, either, but looks marvelous in a full-length mink coat and what will soon be known to America as his courtroom sunglasses. Of all the Cowboys involved in Fat Mikey Bertolini's signing, the only one willing to be interviewed is Darryl (Moose) Johnston, the team's popular fullback.

The whole scene has the charm of a peep show. And the National Football League takes no part against these players showing up for an event run by a hood like Bertolini. The league does not endorse these things, or encourage them, and mostly wishes they would go away. But it knows it can't stop them, either. Paul Tagliabue, his fear of courtrooms as powerful as ever, worries more about legal actions that might be initiated if he ever tried to prevent his ballplayers from showing up to sign their names and make this easy money.

But the saddest pictures of all do not involve the players grubbing around for extra money. The saddest pictures involve the fans, so many of them fathers and sons, grubbing around the grubbers. There is a young couple in the line, in their mid-twenties. The husband is as excited as a ten-year-old at the prospect of getting this close to Aikman and Irvin and Smith and the rest of them. He proudly says that his basement at home is a shrine to the Dallas Cowboys, autographed pictures and balls and posters and helmets.

These are the same Cowboys who wouldn't give this man the time of day unless he coughed up $100 first.

The fans, though, keep moving up in the lines, wearing their Cowboys T-shirts, jackets, caps, gloves, scarves. Grubbing for the grubbers. Stars in their eyes and stars sitting at the tables in front of them. The people move up to the front of the line finally, and the players don't even look at them. You know who these fans are? They are just more people put on this earth to take care of ballplayers, past and present. They wait for hours and then the ballplayers don't even make goddamned eye contact with them. There is no more demeaning sight in all of sports than this one in Summit, New Jersey, on a Saturday afternoon, watching these people whose self-worth is somehow tied in to some sort of contact with the champions of the football world.

Then we turn around and wonder why there is never a reality check for the modern athlete unless he gets hurt. Even though the reason is simple enough: There is no reality. Then the fools who run the sport of baseball turn around and try to tell us that the sport can improve its image with fans by encouraging players to sign more autographs. The fools should show up some Saturday afternoon in some place like the Garden State Convention Center and then decide if they think autographs are some miracle drug for sports.

There was a time once, before autographs passed over from

being a sweet hobby to big business, when collecting was taken out of the hands of children and turned over to the hustlers, when autographs really did mean something. Not because you had Joe DiMaggio's signature, or Mickey Mantle's, or Willie Mays's. But because DiMaggio or Mantle or Mays gave you that signature. But that was a time when sports like baseball still felt like a pastime in this country, instead of some sick obsession. Now everything can be bought. Nothing feels genuine.

The people in the lines pay the exorbitant ticket prices, they pay their cable bills, they buy the Pay-Per-View fights, they buy all the sneakers and T-shirts and jackets and caps. They watch the games. They join the fantasy leagues when even the reality leagues aren't enough for them. Then they are willing to pay again to have a few moments alone with their heroes.

They show up to feed the fantasy that sports cares about them as much as they care about sports.

You know what the Cowboys fans are really doing on this day? Buying into the illusion that their team loves them back. The athlete is willing to let them do it, for a price. Fat Mikey Bertolini, a perfect guy for a scene like this, puts the show on. And legitimate agents like Leigh Steinberg—he represents Aikman and just about every other important quarterback in the NFL—send their boys off with their blessing. And looks like a bit of a pimp himself.

The 1989 Atlantic City show that caused so much legal trouble for so many involved was built around the eleven living members of baseball's 500-home-run club. Hongach, Bertolini's former partner, said at Bertolini's plea hearing that he paid an agent for Mickey Mantle $27,000 in cash. Gerald McMahon, an attorney for a man who gave the cash to the players involved, told *Sports Illustrated* that Mantle made about $175,000 that weekend. Mantle's attorneys have always disputed that figure.

If it wasn't that much for the late Mickey Mantle, it was close enough. Annually, this is now a $2 billion business in this country. Going into the 1996 baseball season, a ball signed by Cal Ripken, Jr., was worth $109. A basketball card signed by Michael Jordan was worth about the same. A bat signed by Ripken went for $449, a helmet for $169. A signed card from Ripken was worth $89. Ripken, by the way, refuses to do card shows, to show up and sign for cash. But he does do bulk signings. Over the course of an average season, Ripken will eventually sign about 8,000 baseballs. There are other stars who sign as many as 40,000.

We have to stop paying them to sign.

Or we'll never stop paying in sports.

My oldest son, now nine, collects baseball cards and basketball cards.

Basketball cards mostly. Every Saturday, he takes his allowance and we go to one of the card stores near our home, and he buys a new pack of cards. When I was growing up, collecting baseball cards myself, there were just Topps cards and that was it. Now the shelves are filled with different brand names: Upper Deck and Flair and Fleer. He is as excited to open a pack and find Michael Jordan in there as I was in the late 1950s and early 1960s to open a pack of Topps cards and find Mantle inside.

But already, at his age, trading with his friends, I can see the whole thing changing. There are now all these magazines—the one I see in his hands most often is called the *Beckett Basketball Monthly*—telling the kids how much the cards are worth. Once a Mantle card had value for me because it was Mantle. Now I hear my boy, who loves sports the way I did at his age, who races downstairs in the morning and puts on ESPN's *SportsCenter* the way he once did cartoons, on the phone talking about a rookie card of Shaquille O'Neal, and how much it is worth.

Already, they are using money as a way of keeping score in sports the way everybody else does.

I keep telling him that card collecting is a hobby, not a business.

I have no idea whether he is listening to me or not.

Chapter Eleven

BABES IN TOYLAND

Nine-year-olds.

Nine-year-olds, twelve-year-olds, eighteen-year-olds.

Colleges, at least the ones that have become football and basketball factories, take in more and more marginal kids as a way to keep the factory going and the money coming in. The fans don't care, the school administration doesn't care, the sneaker companies now funding some big-time college programs don't particularly care, as long as the team keeps winning. In a year, Lawrence Phillips and Christian Peter will be forgotten in the Nebraska program, until Tom Osborne, the sanctimonious coach, recruits another sex offender and Phillips and Peter become frames of reference. Osborne even acts offended when the Patriots don't give Peter a job, and announces he is kicking NFL scouts off campus.

The deceit used to exist in sports that even when athletes were just using a school and a scholarship as a way of being trainees for the pros, they had to learn something in college, that even a little education, in a classroom, on a campus, was better than none.

Now there are high school basketball players who are looking at even one year of college as a waste of time. A Chicago high school kid named Kevin Garnett goes straight from his high school to the Minnesota Timberwolves of the NBA and signs a contract for millions, and that contract, and Garnett's success as a rookie, sends a current of electricity, a hot ripple, all the way through every college basketball program in the country and right into the high schools.

Where another Garnett is thinking: Where's mine?

And there is nothing the NBA can do to stop Kevin Garnett, because there isn't a court anywhere which is going to stop an eighteen-year-old kid from going out to earn a living. Professional tennis has a rule that says you can't turn pro before the age of fourteen, but even that would never stand up to a serious challenge from the parents of a thirteen-year-old or a twelve-year-old who are in a hurry to rush a kid into the game, steal her youth, ruin her life, and make everybody filthy rich in the process.

(Hello, Mr. Capriati. Hello, Mrs. Capriati. Hear from Jennifer lately?)

No one can stop parents in tennis and no one can stop them in gymnastics, either. It starts even earlier in gymnastics than it does in tennis. The parents drop off these sad-looking little girls at the gym when they are eight and nine years old, and it is the same as dropping off a normal childhood, all in the name of a dream about an Olympic gold medal that the parents and gymnastic coaches make sound lofty and important, even as they are turning it seamy instead. (The little girls of gymnastics, even when they make it to the Olympics, even when some injured Dickens character like Kerri Strug thrills the country the way she did at the Atlanta Olympics of 1996, are the saddest creatures in sports. At the Barcelona Olympics of 1992, I was standing with my friend Hubert Mizell of the *St. Petersburg Times* as we watched some medal-winning gymnasts come down off the medal platform. Mizell stared at them a long time and finally said, "Now they get to go back to their room and celebrate by eating a cornflake.") Parents of swimmers are the same way, in a sport where you can often be a has-been at the age of sixteen or eighteen. Hockey boys and baseball boys go straight from high school to some minor-league bus if they think college can do nothing for them. Wayne Gretzky was in the World Hockey Association, scoring goals like crazy, when he was seventeen.

So the corruption of sports begins younger and younger as the prizes get bigger and bigger. There are no real child-labor laws in sports, amateur and professional—and who the hell can tell the difference sometimes?—and there aren't going to be. And there is less and less time, when the athletes are very young, to teach them anything about values. So it is as if they are given some sort of drive-through course in values and boundaries and respect, all the while watching how the big boys of professional sports behave, when they do behave.

Mostly, they are on their way to the money.

It's a wonderful world.

Here is how it looks in the spring of 1996, at Lower Merion High School, outside Philadelphia. Here is a look at sports the way it is now and the way it is going to be in the future, the bleachers of the gymnasium at Lower Merion full of well-to-do sixteen- and seventeen-year-old kids. There are no hardship cases in this gym, there aren't many hardscrabble stories like Michael Irvin's, kids who come out of a household that has sixteen brothers and sisters.

This is just the high school division of Big Sports, the kids there to celebrate one of their own, a seventeen-year-old named Kobe Bryant. Bryant is the son of a former National Basketball Association journeyman, Joe (Jellybean) Bryant, who left college early to join the pros, on his way to a forgettable and mediocre career. The Bryant family had issued a press release a couple of days before. They had scheduled this press conference at the Lower Merion gym. The whole thing was like a party, more festive than a goddamned county fair. There are fifteen news cameras in the gym. There is supposed to be a lot of suspense, too, as Kobe Bryant makes an announcement about whether or not he plans to enter college in the fall, or go straight to the pros.

There is no suspense.

Kobe Bryant is this year's Kevin Garnett.

At 2:30 in the afternoon, as promised, Bryant rubs his chin in mock contemplation and says, "I have decided to skip college and take my talent to the NBA."

The kids in the gym erupt into applause, as if this kid, in his elegant clothes and his hip, Michael Irvin shades—maybe he thought they looked cool when Irvin was on his way into the courthouse a few weeks before—had just announced that none of them had to go to college, either, that they could skip the whole thing and sign million-dollar contracts themselves and never have to crack another book the rest of their lives.

It is as if Kobe Bryant is a poster boy on this day for the way things really are in college sports, even as he announces he doesn't need college sports. He tells the news cameras and all the reporters in the gym that he had even consulted with Kevin Garnett before making his final decision. In so doing, he gives us a glimpse of the real value system we have going right now. Not the value system we want. The value system that *is*. This is how wisdom is passed on now. Not from parent to child. Not from coach to player.

The nineteen-year-olds tell the seventeen-year-olds what's really up.

For Kobe Bryant, Kevin Garnett is a wise old basketball elder, sitting around the fire, counting his money, looking very cool in a new pair of high-tops.

David Stern, who is supposed to be the biggest, most powerful, and most famous sports commissioner in history, can't do a thing with high school kids. If some high school football player wants to be Kevin Garnett or Kobe Bryant someday, Paul Tagliabue isn't going to be able to stop that kid, either. For years and years, the colleges were like farm systems for pro basketball and pro football. The leagues didn't even have to support them, just waited for the kids to develop, and then brought them in after four years at Nebraska, or Notre Dame, or wherever.

Then the rules changed in basketball, and "hardship" cases started coming out of college early, and then the same thing happened in football. Now a couple of high school basketball players, and they sure won't be the last, are just beating the NBA at its own games. And even the kids who decided to give college a try are now leaving after their freshman and sophomore years. A few weeks after Bryant made his announcement at Lower Merion, Allan Iverson, a freshman who had become a star at Georgetown despite serving some jail time for a high school brawl, announced he was making himself available for the NBA draft.

Iverson, who had been seen in previous weeks driving around a leased Mercedes whose value was estimated at around $130,000, said that he felt he had to do this as a way of supporting the son of his unwed girlfriend.

There you go, another single parent just trying to get by.

With his agent, David Falk, sitting there on the podium with him.

Where the hell is Norman Rockwell when you really need him?

Stephon Marbury, a Georgia Tech freshman guard, had come out early in April. But then Marbury had told friends from the time he came out of high school in Brooklyn that it was going to be one year for him of college and then out. Why were they all doing this? For the same reason that Willie Sutton robbed banks: because the NBA is where the money is.

The economy, stupid.

In 1995, the first four picks of the NBA draft were sophomores: Joe Smith of Maryland, Antonio McDyess of Wake Forest, Rasheed Wallace of North Carolina, Jery Stackhouse of North Carolina.

No. 5 was Garnett.

This is why the best college ball anywhere is now being played in the NBA. The best college basketball show isn't at the Final Four, it's the rookie game during the NBA's All-Star weekend blast. These kids get very tired very fast of doing what is basically charity work for major universities, of watching everybody get rich except them. The athletic department gets rich, the coaches get rich, making a ton of dough for sneakers the kids wear. The stands are full and the television money keeps rolling in, and after a year, or two, the kids want to make their score. They also get very tired, very fast, of hearing people such as ESPN's Dick Vitale and CBS's Billy Packer shill relentlessly for the coaches in college basketball, making the coaches out to be the stars, as if Kentucky's Rick Pitino is playing Syracuse's Jim Boeheim a game of one-on-one for the national championship. There isn't a major college coach in the country in front of whom Vitale and Packer haven't genuflected.

And occasionally done a little more than that.

Then these guys wring *their* hands when star players leave school early and hurt their game. And their ratings. In so doing, they sound like the biggest and loudest phonies we have going in sports television.

I know, that's saying a lot.

It isn't just economists, in the words of Mario Cuomo, who survive on elegant bullshit.

These kids don't need a college education to see through this kind of crap, from the coaches, from the announcers, from the people filling their pockets because of an audience the players supply to them, because of their product. At the last Final Four, staged at the Meadowlands in New Jersey, I asked Packer why he spends so much time talking about the coaches.

"Because they're the product we have that people know the best," Packer said.

This was on Friday at the Continental Airlines Arena, the day before the national semifinals. All four teams practice for an hour on Friday, and fans can come in for free. In other years, I have seen arenas packed with people on this day in college basketball, almost like a holiday in the sport, cheering every dunk. This year there are perhaps 5,000 people in the house. Some of that can be blamed on a snowstorm that had hit the New York–New Jersey area overnight. But there was something more going on this year, something more than the weather, even with the sport's showcase event being held about seven miles from midtown Manhattan. The ratings were way down in college basketball, and so was interest in the postseason pageant now known as March Madness.

"The players come and go," Packer continued, "but the coaches stay. So my theory is, Sell the coaches."

Beautiful. He sells the coaches on television, and at the same time, he is really selling the most talented kids on the idea of getting the hell out and getting to the NBA as fast as possible. The coaches get bigger and bigger and the star quotient in college basketball gets lower and lower. Grant Hill, Duke graduate, now a star with the Detroit Pistons, was the last great player in college basketball to play all four years. People now wonder how long it will be before they see someone of Hill's talent and stature go the distance.

No one really believes that Kevin Garnett and Kobe Bryant are going to start some huge wave of high school kids making an early move to the NBA. But soon there will be a junior coming out. And the danger in all this is that more and more high school kids will look at the likes of Garnett and Bryant, see Iverson and Marbury bailing out of college after their freshman years, and think: Why should I even waste time studying now? It used to be that kids worried about grades in high school because they needed them, at least some of the time, to get into the college of their choice. The idea of college cheapens now for high school freshman and sophomores, as does the idea of learning.

And we will be sending more and more talented dopes into the pros.

Kobe Bryant, by the way, is hardly a dope. He had good grades at Lower Merion and a combined score of 1080 on his SATs and could have gotten into any good school, and good basketball program, of his choosing. That is why his father was asked this question after the press conference in his son's gym:

"Why the rush?"

"Well," Joe Bryant said, "we did promise everybody a decision by late April or early May."

"No," Joe Bryant was told. "Why the rush to the pros?"

The question made him mad.

"This isn't rushed," he said. "This is his dream. When everybody is at the bars, he'll be back studying."

Sure he will. Of course he will. You can just hear the conversation now: "I'm sorry, Alonzo, I can't go club-hopping with you tonight, I've only got twenty pages to go in *The Brothers Karamazov.*"

Of course, everything was not perfect in Kobe Bryant's world, what was left of his high school life, on April 29, 1996. He admitted in the gym at Lower Merion High that he did not yet have a shoe contract or an agent.

That came three weeks later.

You know what they say around the NBA, right?

I love this game.

SO WHAT DO WE DO?

So how do we stop more and more of these kids from turning what should have been their freshman year of college into their rookie season in the NBA?

The NBA isn't going to get any help from the law, from the courts, because sports never seems to get much help there. Maybe there isn't going to be a mass exodus from the high school prom to the draft, one Kobe after another. But you had to wonder what high school juniors all over America were thinking when they watched Bryant sign his Adidas contract.

And it gets better than that.

Doesn't it always in sports?

A couple of weeks after the Knicks lost a tough five-game playoff series to the Chicago Bulls, Dave Checketts, the president of the Knicks—and president of Madison Square Garden—got a call from a man named Howard Rubenstein, one of the most famous and most powerful public relations flacks in New York City. If you're keeping score at home, this was right around the time of Kobe Bryant's high school graduation, suddenly a trifle in his young and exciting life, long before Bryant would be drafted by the Charlotte Hornets, then traded to the Lakers.

Why, you ask, was famous flack and spin doctor and lifelong hustler Rubenstein calling?

He told Checketts he wanted just the right setting for Kobe's announcement.

"Kobe's already made his announcement," Checketts said.

"No," Rubenstein said, "the announcement about his new line of clothing."

Checketts said, "Excuse me."

"We thought the Garden would give the proper ambiance . . ." Rubenstein said.

Checketts just laughed. About something that is no laughing matter, to his team or anybody else's. Because all of a sudden, high school kids—and their parents—have not only figured out a way to beat college basketball at *its* game, but the pros at *their* game. All of a sudden, there is a rookie salary cap in the league, because everybody got sort of tired of people like Glenn (Big Dog) Robinson, coming out of Purdue and looking for his own $100 million contract in the league before he'd ever dunked the ball.

Looking for 100 mil and ending up at around 70 or so.

(Another ballplayer set for life that no NBA fan has yet bought a ticket to watch.)

So these kids look at it this way: Even if I have to sit on the bench for two years, even three years, I'm still making a million a year, or two million, or three at a time when I would be looking over the shoulder in college every time somebody wants to give me a free meal.

So how do you get them to college for even a couple of years in a climate like this?

Pay them.

Not because we somehow have to preserve the glorious system of college basketball. College basketball has been using these kids for years, allowing itself to be a fabulously lucrative form of basketball minor league, telling itself the whole time how valuable basketball scholarship is for these fine young scholar-athletes. What a fine trade-off that is for everybody.

Sure it is.

No, I've always believed that these kids, even if they don't get Rhodes Scholar grades the way someone like Bill Bradley did in the old days, are better off being in a college setting, even for a little while, than if they never go at all. Half an education, in this case, being better than no education. So pay them to go to psych class.

Maybe you can't get close to what they would make in the NBA, sitting on that bench, learning their trade. But maybe they can be convinced that two years of being a college star, and getting paid pretty good for it, is just as good. And a better life at eighteen or nineteen.

Just make sure you pay them real money.

I always love it when I see someone like Billy Packer or Dick Vitale saying that, yes, we agree that college needs to pay the players now.

(As a way of keeping them in school. Maintaining college basketball's status as a big deal. And keeping people like Packer and Vitale in their seats on the gravy train of sports.)

Give them $25,000 a year, they say.

Hey, we'll give them $50,000 if we have to.

Wow.

It's not enough, boys. Not anymore.

Maybe the only way to do the job properly is to bring the sneaker companies into it. If Nike wants to put a basketball team on scholarship, as it routinely does, make sure the players start getting their cut. They don't get the television money and they don't get a share of the gate receipts. It is clear that free sneaks don't carry quite the thrill they did in the old days. So let's get everything out in the open, with Nike and with the schools and with the NCAA and with the players, and finally cut those players in.

If Nike wants to be in a college basketball business, don't just pay the school and don't just pay the coaches. If the school gets a million, or whatever it is, matching funds go into a fund for those players. Policed by the NCAA as rigorously as it polices every infraction it can find from coast to coast. If you want to put a salary cap in there, go ahead. But with the biggest stars coming out of high school, schools can pay them. Say it is a million and say it is the next Kobe Bryant. Decide how much you can afford to pay him, and get a couple of other good recruits.

If the next Bryant thinks he can get a better deal from UCLA or Kentucky, that will be his right.

The only condition is that the player must stay two years in college and maintain his eligibility, which means go to class.

Throw in a bonus of a million dollars if he actually stays around long enough to graduate. Maybe the schools, who know full well the kind of revenue star players and star teams generate, from Nike and television and gate receipts, will want to kick in even more than that for a Michael Jordan, a Patrick Ewing, a Grant Hill.

I know, I know. If we do institute a salary cap like this, schools will be finding ways around it in about fifteen minutes, the players will be talking about striking, the fans of college sports will be saying they're mad as hell.

And before long, some seven-foot seventh grader will have his own sneaker line.

Chapter Twelve

PIT BULLS

The weaker the union, the stronger the sport.

But more deep labor talk later.

The two most powerful forces in sports over the last thirty years have been free agency and the modern sports union. Deciding which was greater for the players is like trying to decide between Barry Bonds and Ken Griffey, Jr. Free agency would never have come about in baseball if Marvin Miller hadn't come along in the 1960s to build the Major League Baseball Players Association with his bare hands. But without free agency, which came nearly a decade after Miller came into baseball, without the clout and economic empowerment it gave individual players, the collective clout of baseball players would have scared no one.

So it really did become the most formidable and historic combination—the freedom to organize combined with the freedom to move around—since Jackie Robinson and the Brooklyn Dodgers in 1946. Every twenty years or so, there would be an earthquake in baseball that would change things forever.

When Miller came along in 1967, the minimum salary for a major league player was $6000, and that was $1000 more than it had been in 1947. There had been some form of a players' union going all the way back to 1947, but no one really paid any attention to it, and the owners continued to hold a hammer over all the players, from stars such as Sandy Koufax, who had to hold out, along with Don Drysdale, in 1966 to get himself up to a salary of $100,000, to the guy at the end of the bench making the $6000 and just looking to hang on.

Again: Miller came along and made the whole thing between the players and the owners, at the start anyway, into a fair fight. That isn't the problem, at least in hindsight. The problem is that in the years since Miller showed up on the scene, as salaries have climbed into the millions and the average salary in baseball has grown to $400,000, what started out to be a fair fight became a lopsided fight for the players. The modern sports union, and that really means baseball's union, because it is the model for all the other sports, has not just made its members rich, beefed up their pensions, given players their rightful share of television money and merchandising money, improved their medical coverage, blah blah blah. It has effectively taken over the running of the game, especially now that baseball's owners have eliminated the job of commissioner. (And things have been going great for them without one, right?) While the owners have been unable to get together on anything—other than their notion in 1994 that if they forced another strike, they could crush the union once and for all—the players' solidarity has become something that must make the boys at the Teamsters weep with envy.

In all of baseball's work stoppages in the 1970s and '80s and '90s, not a single player has crossed a picket line. There are always players making noises about doing that. Nobody ever crosses. Nobody ever breaks ranks. This isn't the air traffic controllers, there's no threat that there won't be jobs for most of them when the strike or lockout is over. The ballplayers, no matter how much money they lose, are never really working without a net. Still they hang together, every single time. When NFL players went out on strike in 1987, they were full of big talk, and then after a couple of weeks, players started crossing the line in such numbers—led by their stars—that you thought you were watching the start of the Boston Marathon. Never happens in baseball. Never even close. First under Miller—the Samuel Gompers of sports—and now under Donald Fehr. Their loyalty to the union and to each other looks like blind loyalty sometimes. But the bastards stay the course, you have to give them that.

You pick a fight with one ballplayer, you pick a fight with all of them.

Every time the owners have picked a fight with them since Marvin Miller came along to hijack the gravy train, the owners have gotten their asses kicked.

There was a fight once between Mike Tyson and Michael Spinks, before Tyson went off to the big house for being a very bad boy. Spinks was the light-heavyweight champ at the time and had never lost, and there were a lot of people who thought he might have the same kind of shot against Tyson that Billy Conn had against Joe Louis in the old days.

Fight didn't last a round.

The bell rang, and as soon as Spinks started moving in Tyson's direction, he looked more scared than one of the actress girls in one of those *Friday the 13th* movies. Then Tyson proceeded to drop a piano on Spinks and put him out of his misery.

That's what the players always did to the owners, all the way until the strike of 1994, when the owners, for the first time, did not get Spinksed. One time, the owners held out for fifty-five days before they went down; that was their record before '94. It happened during the 1981 season. Even when that one was over, Miller made them look tamer than a house puppy.

And I defended the union every bloody step of the way, cheered them on every time they kicked the owners square in the balls. Because if you were picking sides in those days, you couldn't go with the owners. The players had gotten screwed for much too long and the owners still looked as mean and petty as ever, and Miller was the one making all the sense. Besides, in the early days of free agency, none of us watching baseball could figure out why the owners had a bitch. It seemed that free agency had created a tremendous boom for everyone between the middle of the '70s to the middle of the '80s. So we all told the owners to shut up and get out and give the players what they wanted and play ball.

We felt braver than Sergeant York doing it, I might add. We all thought the players were in a perpetual state of grace.

Time passed. The players kept winning. And over time, those of us in the media still cheering this rout finally made the biggest mistake you can make covering sports: We started to think like players.

As if we were all on the same team.

Good guys on one side, owner scum on the other. And why not? The players were just protecting their hard-earned rights. Right? Even though the owners were screaming bloody murder every time they walked away from the bargaining table, everybody on both sides sure seemed to be getting rich. Television money kept going up, attendance kept going up, salaries were going through the goddamned roof. The guys running the players' union were like kids who'd taken over the principal's office. No commissioner was tough enough to take them on. Or take them out. The players were always ready to fight the world; the owners would always go into a room and fight with each other.

When the owners tried to fight back, they did it illegally, with collusion. That was in the middle 1980s, under Commissioner Peter Ueberroth's watch. The owners couldn't do anything with the players at the bargaining table, so they decided to break the baseball law, and agree among themselves not to sign free agents. They were about as clever doing this as Marv and Harry in the *Home Alone* movies, and of course they got caught. It ended up costing them, as a group, hundreds of millions of dollars.

They were so greedy in these years, so hopelessly arrogant, we missed something.

The union was becoming more arrogant.

Turning into the pit bulls of sport.

They didn't just think they were right sometimes. They thought they were right all the time. The owners were wrong. All the time. Not only wrong, but crooked. So, over time, the union, because it had never lost, because it had never really been challenged, because it absolutely scared commissioners and owners and league presidents and even umpires to death, became another monster of sports.

The union didn't care about the future of the sport, and it certainly did not care about us. It said it did, of course. It said it was protecting our interests as soon as it got through protecting its players.

Another crock.

The union doesn't care about the fans, doesn't want a real partnership with the owners, doesn't worry about looking down the road. The union had the hammer now, after all the years of the twentieth century when the owners had the hammer, and they were going to use it. They wanted the owners to sit when they were told to sit, stand when they were told to stand. Then roll over and play dead on payday.

Sometimes this happens in Big Sports, and it happens on my watch:

Things that start out looking like a more wonderful idea than cable TV turn to garbage. And real sports heroes such as Marvin

Miller, when you see what they have wrought, come up looking like villains. Why? Because the Major League Baseball Players Association wanted it all, that's why. Because Miller and his successors did their jobs so well—with all of us in the media cheering them on—that they turned into terrorists.

Didn't just want their fair share.

Wanted it all.

There once was a famous Hollywood agent named George Chasin, now deceased. Among Chasin's clients was Jacqueline Susann. And there was a time when Chasin made such a killing for Miss Susann on one of her novels that he offered this insane-sounding—but ultimately wise—lament:

"I made too good a deal."

Chasin explained: "I didn't leave anything on the table. And you've got to leave something on the table. If you don't, everybody except your client walks away pissed off."

You've got to leave something on the table.

Another verse to remember, as much for sports as for the movies. Tattoo it on your upper arm as the ballplayers do, if you're afraid you might forget. Only the baseball union never leaves anything on the table. The individual agents never leave anything on the table. The ballplayers have gotten fabulously wealthy because the table always ends up as clean as the top of Michael Jordan's head. It is why Miller and Fehr are the best friends any ballplayer ever had.

And as much the enemy to us as anybody in sports.

I am sitting in the office of a Guy Who Knows.

You would certainly know his name from sports if I told it to you. But I'm not going to tell it to you. Suffice to say, the Guy Who Knows has a job that brings him into play with everything and everybody in Big Sports: owners, players, commissioners, agents, unions leaders, network presidents. He has been on the inside, and in play, with all of them. He understands the action of sports as an insider better than anybody I know.

We are having our conversation in the spring of 1996. In the last couple of weeks, Nick Van Exel of the Lakers has shoved an official, Magic Johnson has bumped one, Marge Schott has been under fire for wanting to play her Opening Day game after the death of umpire John McSherry, then for giving a television interview to ESPN about how Hitler had some very good ideas at the beginning, it was only later that the little guy went off the rails a little bit. Shaquille O'Neal, after taking two games off following the death of his grandmother, won't tell his coach, Brian Hill, if he is planning to show up for a nationally televised game between the Magic and the Bulls, and finally waltzes into the Orlando Arena as the ball is being thrown up; maybe we should have known Shaq was on his way to the Lakers right there. There is a sexual-harassment charge made against Ken Behring of the Seattle Seahawks. Michael Irvin is in the news after being in the motel room. The FBI announces that it is searching Alonzo Mourning's Washington residence for drugs, but says Mourning is not part of the investigation.

A woman in Chicago says that Mike Tyson has sexually assaulted her, though no official charges will ever be filed by the Chicago police. A woman at the China Club in New York City says that Anthony Mason of the Knicks slugged her, though that looks dubious, and there are no charges there, either.

Modern sports was just being modern sports, in other words.

So I am talking about all of it with a Guy Who Knows, talking about how all these problems and controversies seem to be falling into our laps on a daily basis, through some sports hole in the ozone. We kick it all around for a while, and finally the guys says, "Do you think people think sports was better in the old days?"

"Depends on their age, but yes, I believe they generally think the old days were better."

"How far back?"

I tell him the 1950s, but point out that, for all the romance and nostalgia about the '50s, it was a time when pro sports in this country were still mostly white, players couldn't move around, the salary structure was ridiculous, the owners had the hammer.

"You're right about the wrong stuff," he said. "But even when you look back at what was wrong in the '50s and what's happened since, where have the major improvements been?"

I thought about it and finally said, "With the players."

"Bingo. Things have gotten better for the players, but let me ask you a question: Has sports gotten better?"

"No."

"It's why I don't think the biggest problem in sports is the owners," he says.

"So you think it's the players?" I said.

"No," he says. "It's their unions."

"Now, hear me out," he continues, "before you say I just sound like some greedy owner. I'm not looking to wipe out unions. I'm not saying that players shouldn't have someone protecting their rights and their interests. But it's gone so far past that, it's ridiculous. The modern athlete gets all the protection of any union member, and then he is allowed to negotiate individually, for these huge salaries. It's all they care about: top dollar, for every single member. They do not care about any of the things the fan cares about. They care about their members. Period. And then, when somebody comes to them and says a sport is in real trouble, they say it's a lie. If they're told the books can prove it, the union says the books have been cooked. And too often the media plays right along with them.

"Players want the freedom to move, to be unrestricted free agents, and it never occurs to them that all this movement is bad for the stability of their business."

I say to him, "What would you change?"

"Whatever cut of the total revenue of the sport the players are getting, I'd offer them an even bigger cut. Fifty-two percent, fifty-five percent. Even sixty percent. Then I'd hand it over to them and say, 'Now you whack it up among your players in a way you think is fair. Give the stars their fair share, give the guys in the middle their fair share. I'd make it as lucrative for stars to stay where they are as it is for them to move around. Because what I want in return is less free agency. Because players have to stop moving around the way they do. Somewhere along the line, unions finally have to realize that it's bad for business. Because every time another player leaves another team, sports loses something right here."

He points to his heart, then continues.

"These people, and I'm talking about sports unions and their members, better wake up to something. They have to give something up occasionally to make the kind of money they make, live the kind of life this sport and all the other sports allow them to live. And one of the things they've got to give up is the freedom to move around the way they do. Because it is pissing off their audience. And it's bad for business. And it's going to hurt all of us in the end."

Voice crying in the wilderness.

Baseball's union is the strongest, by far, and the sport that is in the lousiest shape as we come to the end of the century, the one coming off a work stoppage that ended up costing players and owners nearly a billion dollars, is baseball.

Stronger the union, weaker the sport.

It doesn't let the owners off the hook for anything, doesn't absolve them of their sins against sports, it's just the way things are.

Over the years, the ego of the union has been fed as surely as the egos of the athletes have been fed. In fact, the union has turned into some star player: imperious, greedy, fighting every suspension, every drug violation, fighting the owners for every last nickel as if it were still 1966.

Only it's not 1966 anymore.

Ballplayers aren't underprivileged anymore, they're goddamned overprivileged, and overindulged, and often overpaid. Things happen to be going very well for professional athletes, and every dispute between them and the boss doesn't have to be treated like the apocalypse anymore. Only that's the way the unions play it. This isn't just baseball we're talking about now, it's all the sports. They all say they want to compromise, but they only do that as a last resort. Their idea of leaving something on the table is leaving a tip for the maid. Marvin Miller never really lost, and now Donald Fehr, his successor, is obsessed with Miller's shadow, obsessed that anything he could do in front of his players and the owners could be perceived as weakness. So Fehr held his people together, held the line during the strike that started in August of '94 and lasted all the way to the end of spring training in '95, held that line as well as Miller ever did.

Only this time, the players got their asses kicked, too.

When the owners didn't punch themselves in the nose, Fehr showed that his real negotiating strategy—other than crossing his arms and shaking his head no—was to have no negotiating strategy. The owners lost a ton? So did Fehr's players. Whatever kind of deal Fehr would eventually make for his members, he had presided over such a major financial calamity for so many of them he should have been fired. For the money Selig, the CEO of baseball, lost for himself and his fellow owners, he should have been fired, too. Twenty years into free agency, these assholes couldn't figure out a way to cut up a $2 billion pie, and stood in front of the whole country, all of them with their pants around their ankles.

In sports, this is what passes for progress.

During the baseball strike, I interviewed President Clinton one night. He had tried to get both sides to the White House, to bang their thick heads together and get a solution in the spring of 1995 before the ruined spring training, and even the President of the

United States couldn't get through to these people. A few weeks later, this is what Clinton said about the experience:

"A small group of men bickering about how to cut up a billion-dollar pie, and being unable to do it."

The President paused and said, "It sounds a little bit like the federal government."

So which sport has the best collective bargaining agreement right now, the relationship between management and labor that seems to work the best?

The National Hockey League.

Number four out of the four major sports, with no prospects of ever getting out of fourth place. The NHL has undergone a tremendous growth spurt in this country in the 1990s, has a terrific commissioner in Gary Bettman—hired away from the NBA, where he was David Stern's right-hand man—and for the first time has a real national television contract, with Fox. In short, the league is doing the best it can in this country, even though it is a sport that belongs to another country, Canada.

Over the first half of what was supposed to be the 1994–95 season, coming off the tremendous momentum the sport had picked up when the New York Rangers had won their first Stanley Cup in fifty-four years the previous June, the NHL also had a bitter labor dispute. The league had gone more than a year without a new collective bargaining agreement; Bettman had been hired to get one. He was going to get one, even going up against a players' union, led by a former Harvard hockey player named Bob Goodenow, that thought it was the baseball union. He locked the players out from training camp all the way to January, and was prepared to lose the season if he had to. But when a deal was finally struck—even without the salary cap that Bettman (who had helped invent the salary cap for pro basketball) was looking for—it had more elements that made sense than either baseball or basketball or pro football.

Rookie salary cap over the first three years of a player's career.

No unrestricted free agency until a player reaches the age of thirty-two.

No arbitration for the first two seasons after the rookie salary cap.

When a player does become a restricted free agent, a team has the right to match the offer, or receive significant compensation. A $3 million-a-year player, for example, would bring five first-round draft picks in return. And the way the rules are written, it is difficult for a team to make more than one play for that kind of player over the life of that player's contract.

When a player receives an arbitration award, the team to which he belongs has three options: sign him for the full award, sign him for one or two years, or just walk away. In this way, hockey owners aren't slaves to arbitration the way baseball owners are.

(Arbitration, by the way, is a lucrative stopover on the way to free agency. After a certain portion of a player's career, and before he can leave, he can go to arbitration. He submits a figure, the ball club submits a figure. An arbitrator measures the player's stats against all other comparable players, and their salaries. It's like a game show, only you never really lose. You end up with the fabulous money you want, or the less-fabulous money the club offers. And once one .260 hitting shortstop makes a big score, all .260 hitting shortstops then make the same score. The owners have been trying to get this back from the players for years. The players, as you can probably understand, protect it the way they would Mom.)

How did Bettman and his owners get this system? They pulled back on a salary cap that Goodenow said he would never give them. Maybe Bettman thought he could get the cap, maybe he couldn't. But he ended up with a system that drastically reduced player movement, and that was the most important thing of all. He also indicated to Goodenow that he was willing to burn an entire season to get the kind of deal he was after, and if Goodenow could convince his membership that a season out of their lives was worth the fight, then God bless him.

The union walked away from the table acting a lot less tough than when it showed up. Obviously, Bettman has more leverage than someone like David Stern, just because Bettman's stars don't have anywhere near the clout Michael Jordan does, or Shaquille O'Neal. There is no hockey agent with the kind of juice David Falk has in basketball. So no commissioner right now has the kind of juice that Bettman has.

The NHL is a lot better off for that.

Sorry, Marvin.

"All players in sports have to realize something," Bettman said. "They aren't like people in other businesses. They're not doctors, they're not lawyers, they don't have jobs in the media. I'll hear a player say, 'Lawyers get to move around whenever they want to.' And you know what I want to say sometimes? 'Good luck in law school.'"

Chapter Thirteen

AGENTS AND OTHER WEASELS

Which leads us to sports agents.

Sports agents have become a virus in sports, from the smallest shiftiest ones to the self-proclaimed Super Agents (are these like Super Models, by the way? Haven't you always wondered when one of them passes over from plain old model to . . . Super Model!?), such as pro basketball's David Falk and pro football's Leigh Steinberg. Agents, in fact, are just another example of a good idea gone wrong in sports, like unions and free agency and even rock-and-roll music at the ballpark. Once people like these fought a good fight for their clients, much as the unions did. Now they all run around as if they're in training to be Michael Ovitz when Ovitz was running the Creative Artists Agency, as if their job isn't just to make the biggest possible score, but to shape the future of sports, and franchises. And the only problem with that is that most agents, a huge majority of them, don't have the soul for it, the vision, the perspective, the humanity, or the knowledge of sports.

Most of them are weasels on the sports landscape, is what they are.

No matter how much money they can command for their clients, no matter how they can grab headlines with their demands, there is something very, very important to remember about sports agents, super or otherwise:

In the end, they are nobodies.

They do not enrich sport, elevate sport, make sport better for anyone, certainly not for fans. They have no art, or genius. They cannot dunk a ball or hit a home run or run down the football field with the ball dodging tacklers. And their asses are never, ever on the line the way an athlete's is, or even an owner's. As bulletproof as both players and owners like to think they are, both sides know they are eventually held accountable for their actions, good or bad. It doesn't mean we can control what happens to them. It doesn't mean we can get rid of them if they don't deliver, even though there have certainly been instances when fans felt as if they at least drove a ballplayer out of town.

Agents add nothing to sports except zeroes.

And that's what so many of them are, bless their hearts.

With all that, they are powerful as hell, as big and fat and powerful as the offensive line of the Dallas Cowboys. There isn't a team owner in basketball, a team president, who is ever going to, um, screw with David Falk. (As a matter of fact, maybe we should even change the verb right here and say falk with him. New sports verb.) Because Falk is Michael Jordan. He is Alonzo Mourning. He is Juwan Howard. And Patrick Ewing. He is Kenny Anderson and Dikembe Mutombo. And more. Next to David Stern, Falk is the most powerful man in professional basketball at this time.

And please understand: This has nothing to do with Falk being a great man, or having some grand vision for the game. He doesn't. He is a grifter. His vision is dollar signs. He makes the most money he can for his clients, and that is that, even if Falk always wants to make the whole thing sound like church. Does it make him different from an agent in the movie business, or the book business? Not a whole hell of a lot. We all have agents, and none I know ever mistakes movies or books for the Lawn Tennis Association. They aren't in it for the love of the game.

But the ones in the other fields aren't as dangerous to ticket buyers—in movie theaters, in bookstores—as sports agents are.

Book prices keep going up, no one could ever say they don't. But they are not going through the roof the way fans think prices are in sports. Same with movies. It is more expensive than ever to go to the movies; the price was $8.50 in Manhattan when Tom Cruise, one of those $20 million men, opened in *Mission Impossible*, in the summer of 1996. But the movie prices will stay there for a while, even with Cruise, and Harrison Ford, and Jim Carrey making the kind of money they do.

But I guarantee you that, while I was writing this chapter, some sports team somewhere raised its ticket prices. When Shaquille O'Neal signed with the Lakers, a ticket that sold for $9.50 during the season just ended immediately went to $20. Poof. As if, well, by (Orlando) Magic.

In sports, it never seems to stop, because the salaries never stop. From the beginning of time, certainly from the time the first baseball players were making $100,000 a season, people have asked this questions: Where does it stop? The moon, that's where. And after that, in the words of Buzz Lightyear in *Toy Story*, to infinity and beyond. In a few weeks of the summer of 1996, if you were keeping score at home, you saw Jordan sign a one-year, $25 million contract with the Bulls, Shaq went for $120 million longterm, Alonzo Mourning reportedly went for $112 million in Miami. Juwan Howard first signed a $100 million contract with the Heat, then the league ruled it violated salary-cap rules, and Howard, before even waiting to see how the arbitration about all that came out, immediately signed another $100 million contract with his old team, the Bullets. Two hundred-million contracts in the same month, a new world's record. And Kenny Anderson went for $50 million. Dikembe Mutombo went for $49 million in Atlanta. All but one—Shaq—were represented by Falk.

Who, in the summer of 1996, was only looking to change the salary structure for his clients, and all of basketball, forever.

And who didn't give a damn about what it might do to the sport.

Falk you.

You can see what was happening here. David Stern wasn't the most powerful figure in the NBA anymore. Falk the agent was. The other David. He was setting the agenda here. He was establishing future salary structure in the NBA.

Micky Arison, the Heat owner, was willing—before all the confusion about Juwan Howard's contract—to pay Alonzo Mourning more, much more, for the 1996–97 season than this team earned for the 1995–96 season.

Roll those dice up and down the crap table—and I do mean crap—a few times.

Stern wasn't going to lose sleep over any of this, believe me. If David Stern would lose some sleep, so would Arison's fellow owners. Just not the agent Falk. An agent like this, with his kind of client list, never goes out of business, never has a bad year, never loses. He wins a little or he wins a lot. He speed-dials his way around the league and changes the face of sports as he does it, changes the economy of sports, alters the balance of power, sometimes for a decade.

But there is no accountability for them, ever. It is why the agent does not care about the fans, because the fans have nothing to do with the next deal, the next score. The fans never keep score with an agent the way they do with a ballplayer's scoring average, his batting average, his win-loss percentage. The win-loss column and the stat sheet might not ever make the player sell a Mercedes or

Ferrari, but it doesn't mean they don't hear the boos, listen to the horrible things fans say about them on the radio, twenty-four hours a day.

The fans don't get near the agent, can't touch him. Sports fans know the name David Falk. The sophisticated ones know about his impressive client list. That's it. They can't lay a glove on the sonofabitch. He moves around sports like The Phantom, minus the funny comic-book-hero costume and the cool decoder ring. Most fans would be shocked to find out he's the ordinary-looking bald head in the expensive courtside seats at the United Center in Chicago, watching Jordan, or at Madison Square Garden, watching Ewing.

When Allan Iverson announced he was leaving Georgetown after his freshman year to go to the NBA, it surprised no one to see Falk right there with him. Surprised no one and gave us a warm feeling all over. Falk is in the picture, whether you want him there or not.

Like the Big Sports version of Where's Waldo.

Leigh Steinberg, who is as important a figure in pro football at this time as Falk is in basketball, is different. Steinberg, who seems to have just about every rich, famous NFL quarterback except Slingin' Sammy Baugh on his client list, does not want to hide. Steinberg, in fact, acts as if he is running for some kind of office, as if he wants to be Chief Operating Conscience of sports. Steinberg is the Super Agent as regular guy, even congenial host. He throws a party every year that tries to outdo the legendary and excessive party thrown by the commissioner of the National Football League. Steinberg's party is always crawling not just with his clients, but with a ton of sportswriters and television people. Part of his action is in getting these people on his side. Getting these people to like him has practically become a second career for him.

Steinberg says he does not just go for the top dollar, even as he always does. He does not want to come across as just another successful hustler, but he is. All agents like to set themselves apart from the field. When I was in college, I freelanced a story to *Boston* magazine about the late Bob Woolf, one of the first Super Agents in sports. Woolf was beloved by his clients, and had a fabulous career representing everybody from Carl Yastrzemski to television's Larry King. He was another who would crawl through mortar fire on his belly to give a sportswriter a big hug, if he thought the sportswriter would get his name into print. Woolf's whole deal, even back in the early 1970s, was that he had never solicited a client in his life. He was a Lawyer. The rest of them were Agents. Woolf made "agent" sound cheaper than a thrift shop.

Of course, I made about three phone calls, and it turned out he had recruited clients left and right, all the way into their college dorms.

One kid, I forget his name all these years later, had to lock himself in a bathroom to get away from Woolf.

Steinberg's pitch, not just to his clients, but to all of us, is that he is not just in the business of representing superstar athletes, he is in the business of representing role models. The deceit here—or perhaps just the conceit—is that superstar athletes are still both. Steinberg sells that, and sells it up very big. He also tries desperately to sell the idea that he is not a bottom-line guy, that he worries as much about the quality of life for his players as he does the color of a team's money. That is why when Neil O'Donnell signed with the Jets, Steinberg tried to make it sound as if O'Donnell were going to be happier in Hempstead, Long Island, where the Jets train, than Fletcher Christian was in Tahiti.

Steinberg is another one who says it's not about money when it's always about money.

Steinberg: "Not every single thing in the world is about money. It just isn't. To the extent that someone looking at sports wants to reduce it to that, I mean, they're just missing major, major elements of the reality."

Perish the thought.

Steinberg also disputes the notion that athletes more and more seem to be spinning out of control, incidentally. Wants to play devil's advocate on that one. Says that in the old days, Michael Irvin's arrest would "never have seen the light of day."

Well, there you go.

The problem here isn't Irvin in the hotel room, Irvin with the self-employed models, Irvin with all that dope, sitting there trying to blow his career.

It was the coverage.

Steinberg: "I would maintain that one of the most amazing trends in the twenty years that I've been an agent is how much cleaner athletes' lives have become, how much more ascetic they've become. I would bet that the use of recreation drugs, the use of alcohol, domestic violence, I would bet they are significantly down in every category than they were twenty years ago. It's demonstrably true, I think. The figures have dropped dramatically, even steroid use. So why do fans have the perception that players are behaving in an out-of-control fashion? And the old-fashioned American athlete has been replaced with an alcoholic, girlfriend-beating, cocaine-sniffing [miscreant]? The coverage."

I had a feeling he was working his way up to this being my fault.

But as self-serving as Leigh Steinberg can be—if you don't get passing grades in self-serving, you never make it out of Agent School—there actually are times when he makes as much sense about the problems in sports as anybody around. It won't stop him from bleeding the next team dry when he's got a quarterback to peddle, but Steinberg is smart. He is right that agents have helped the modern athlete manage money better than the athletes of the past ever did. It doesn't mean athletes like Kareem Abdul-Jabbar don't still wake up in Chapter 11 one day. But there are fewer stories about people like Joe Louis ending up as greeters in Las Vegas casinos because most of the money they made from boxing is gone.

It doesn't make any of these guys Jonas Salk, either, which they desperately want to be.

As noble as Dr. Salk, as eager to please as Martha Stewart.

Steinberg: "Athletes are immensely better counseled in their economic affairs than they have ever been."

No argument there.

He goes on to say that he has misgivings about card and memorabilia shows.

Steinberg: "It's not right to do card shows with people of questionable backgrounds. I'm not sure it's right to do card shows at all. . . . I have tremendous misgivings [about the collectibles market], which I've expressed to our athletes, and it's simply this: When I was a kid I walked up to Sandy Koufax, who was my big idol, and he looked back at me. I said, 'My name is Leigh.' He said, 'Hi, Leigh,' and signed my card. And what was special was that he focused on me, even if it was for one second. But now the collectibles business has changed forever the nature of the athletes–fans direct relationship. They're not just fans, they're collectors. Outside every ballpark, huge clusters of people attempt to get athletes' autographs. 'Just sign,' they'll say, 'no name,' which is a sure way to separate collectors from fans. I tell my athletes not to do it. And they say, 'Come on, Leigh, I've got this short career span, I've got to maximize the income.' And I say, 'Wait a second, if you're making six million dollars, isn't maintaining your relationship with the fans more important?'"

It sounds beautiful. But Steinberg is clearly better at selling his ballplayers to football teams than ideas like these to the ballplayers. Troy Aikman, one of Steinberg's richest and most prominent clients, showed up at the Garden State Convention Center after Super Bowl XXX on a Fat Mikey Bertolini scholarship.

Yikes!

And people want to think sports is all about money.

Whatever gets into us?

At the end of the day, though, Steinberg is a sports fan. He lives in the San Francisco area and did lead the fight when the Giants were on the verge of moving to Tampa–St. Petersburg a few years ago. So the Giants remain in San Francisco. If you want to fight to keep teams where they are, you can fight in the Mad as Hell army, even if you don't get to be the general you probably want to be. Steinberg's hand may always be on the wallet of some owner—the way the owner's hand is on our wallet—but sometimes his heart seems to be in the right place. Especially when he talks about the newest owner gadget in sports, which is something called Private Seat Licensing.

Private Seat Licensing is the concept whereby you purchase the right to buy a seat, or two, or four, at your ballpark before you actually buy the tickets. It is much like paying an initiation to get into a country club, which is sort of fitting, since being able to afford sports events is more and more like being a member of a country club. Now people like Bob Kraft of the Patriots say that PSLs are a way to finance new stadiums without looking for tax dollars from the city and state. More cynical sports fans say that sports owners run around looking for new ballparks because they don't have PSLs in their old ones. No matter what fans are paying for their tickets in the old ballparks, the owner starts to feel as if he is giving those seats away. My pal Mitch Albom of the *Detroit Free Press* says that buying a PSL is the equivalent of going into a restaurant and having to pay for the right to read the menu. And yet it goes on all the time now in sports. Because there are enough people willing to pay. And the owner doesn't give a damn how exclusionary his particular country club has become.

Steinberg: "We are imperiling the future of professional sports. A short time frame is not the way to gauge what the impact of this is, private-seat-licensed stadiums filled with people who effectively paid $10,000 a seat. Because what these licenses really do is exclude young people, exclude working-class people, exclude everyone [except the wealthy], really. My father was a schoolteacher, but we got to see sports. These licenses will imperil the ability to create tomorrow's sports fans from the standpoint that if teams are not careful and don't plant the seeds for the future, I'm not sure that someone who has never played sports themselves, has never seen sports in person . . . their entire relationship with sports will be one built around television."

Sometimes there is so much irony in sports, twisted and otherwise, it should make us all laugh. Except that we're too pissed off most of the time. The growth of sports has produced people like Steinberg. The amount of money being poured into sports, from everywhere, means more money is available to Steinberg and his barn full of star quarterbacks. They go for the money, and get it. We've gone all over this. O'Donnell and the joys of Best Available. So they get the money, and the owners look for more money to pay, and so they come up with seat licensing and luxury boxes and a million ways to sell advertising in the new stadiums. And then people like Steinberg stand there when it's all over and say: Seat licensing and luxury boxes are terrible, they're pricing the average fan right into the ozone.

And you know what the great thing is?

Everybody's just doing his job here. Neil O'Donnell did his job, played by the rules. Steinberg did his job with O'Donnell and did his job when he negotiated deals for Drew Bledsoe, the New England Patriots quarterback who got a $4.5 million signing bonus from the Patriots. A couple of years later, Bledsoe gets another $11 million signing bonus on a long-term contract that is worth $42 million. Fair enough, and hurray for Steinberg and Bledsoe. But where does the money come from to pay for Bledsoe? Kraft is looking for seat licensing in his new stadium. Kraft is looking for luxury boxes that would make Donald Trump sick with jealousy.

And soon those fans that Bob Kraft sees in his parking lot every Sunday, those regular fans whose rights he says he must protect because he is the caretaker of a public trust, they'll be gone, replaced by more rich guys and more corporations willing to pay whatever Kraft thinks he can get as a licensing fee.

Maybe you're getting the idea here.

Agents like Leigh Steinberg are able to make a lot of sense about a lot of things in sports. But when they look at you with big, sad eyes and tell you they share your pain, they are about as believable as President Clinton saying he didn't inhale the dope that time when he was at Oxford.

There was a time in the late 1960s when Jim Ringo was the center for Vince Lombardi's great Green Bay Packers teams. Of course, this was before free agency and agents and any kind of real football union. It was just the individual player, with no right to move, with no union muscle, against Lombardi. Which was the same as having no shot at all. But Jim Ringo knew he was a valuable member of Lombardi's team. He thought he deserved a raise. And he decided to bring in a lawyer to negotiate that raise for him.

The day of the meeting arrived.

Ringo went in to talk to Lombardi first.

Then he told Lombardi that he had his lawyer waiting outside.

Lombardi smiled and said, "Give me a couple of minutes, okay?"

"Sure," Jim Ringo said.

It was longer than a couple of minutes. But finally, the lawyer was shown into Lombardi's office.

At which point, Vince Lombardi smiled again and said, "Your client has just been traded to Philadelphia."

Those were the days.

How do we fight back against the agents?

Uh, we don't.

Sorry. As fans we'd have better luck fighting ghosts. They have to be certified by the various unions, but that doesn't help us, that just helps the athletes, because the unions, for the most part, are able to weed out the ones who are excessively slimy, and occasionally even a little bit crooked.

And there is no law that can be passed that says an athlete can't choose a particular agent, or that an agent is allowed to have only a certain number of clients. Or that he is just allowed to have a certain number of clients on the same team. Of all the people in sports, agents are the ones we need the least, and as time passes, they are the ones who seem to have the most power.

This book is supposed to be about solutions, ways for us to fight back. Sorry again.

I will say this, though: In a perfect sports world, there wouldn't be any individual agents. The unions would be like big law firms, and they would hire enough lawyers to do the contract work, and all contracts would go through the union. And there would be a wage scale in place, the one I used to scream about when the baseball owners would suggest one. And the stars would still get their money and the substars would get theirs, and we would have a system where the union was doing exactly what my Guy Who Knows said they should be doing, which is whacking up their share of all the money coming into sport as they saw fit.

I always love it when athletes try to turn another union dispute into the Hormel meatpackers. As if they understand the pain and struggles of all union members everywhere. Maybe in the beginning they did. Maybe that was the way it all shook out when Marvin Miller first came along. Not anymore. Now baseball players, for example, have the protection of the strongest union anywhere, but are allowed to negotiate their own personal contracts. Another place in sports where it is win-win for the players. The salaries of the athletes go up and up, only the average salary of the average fan does not. The gap grows wider and wider. The median income for a family in this country, in 1996, is $37,000.

At a time when Jordan was making $25 million for 82 regular-season games, plus playoffs, in Chicago.

When the Bulls raise their ticket prices, again, as a way of laying off some of those millions, you can bet that David Falk will feel as bad about that as Leigh Steinberg does about seat licensing. They're the type. They're always the first ones into the lifeboats, but they promise to sing "Nearer My God to Thee" real loud.

Other Voices

PAUL WESTPHAL

Paul Westphal, out of the University of Southern California, has had a long and distinguished career in the NBA, first as a player with the Boston Celtics, Phoenix Suns, Seattle SuperSonics, and New York Knicks, then as a coach with the Phoenix Suns. "You're king of the world," I said. "Give me one thing to make the whole thing better."

You want to know what my fantasy league is? It's a league where the real incentives are tied up with winning. Where you've got to win to make all the money, instead of just show up. You've got to win and keep winning to get rich. That's the way it works in professional golf. You've got to win to stay out there. You have to produce and keep producing. Tennis is somewhat the same way. So why can't we have it be that way in the team sports? Why can't it be that way in the NBA? My plan is simple: Pay everybody in the league the same base salary. Just for the purposes of this discussion, say it's half a million a year. That's it, right across the board. But then take the rest of the money *that comes in for the players, whatever that percentage of the gross is, and put all that money in a great big pot. Then have everybody sit down and figure out what a regular-season win should be worth to every team. But you have to win the game to get the money. If your team wins, that money goes into your pot. If your team loses, you get nothing. If a team like the [1995–96] Bulls comes along and wins 72 games, depending on what our math is, they could end up with a pot of $200 million by the end of the season.*

Westphal laughs here.

Then it gets really good, because you have to cut up your share. You go into a room at the end of the year and figure out what everyone has contributed to the team. Say it is the Bulls we're talking about. Michael Jordan might walk away with 50 million. And you know what? He'd be worth it. And no one would complain. Scottie Pippen, depending on his contributions, might walk away with 30 million. Dennis Rodman might get 10. But the guys at the end of the bench, the ones who haven't played and haven't contributed anything except a lot of cheerleading, they might get twenty-five thousand.

Isn't this how law firms do it? The partners go into a room at the end of the year and decide who's been pulling his or her load, who hasn't. Then they start cutting up the firm's profits that way. I'm all for that in sports. I'm all for the stars getting whatever they can get. But I think, just as a fan, not even as a coach or ex-player, I think everybody's sick of seeing everybody get rewarded, whether they've contributed or not. Whether they've won anything or not. I'm one of those people who look at sports and because of the long-term contracts, because of all that, I don't see players fighting to win anymore. So let's try it this way. A million dollars, or whatever it is, if your team wins. Nothing if you lose.

Chapter Fourteen

SPORTS AS THE COTTON CLUB

In an episode of HBO's show *Real Sports* in May of 1996, host Bryant Gumbel suggested that it is "maybe too common" for athletes to "showboat."

Gumbel went on to say this:

"It has, unfortunately, become just as common for writers and broadcasters to bad-mouth those same athletes for being so expressive. What's wrong with that is that, in most cases, those doing the scolding are white and those on the field are black."

Gumbel's solution?

"Keep in mind the social gulf that separates those they're talking about . . . from those they're talking to."

Mr. Gumbel, of course, then the host of the *Today* show as well as *Real Sports*, is an African-American. He also began in sports—a brilliant talent and on-air personality who became the lead announcer at NBC Sports at a young age—and finally became host of the network's coverage of the 1988 Olympics from Seoul, even though he had moved on to *Today* by then. Now he dabbles in sports with a show on HBO that is, along with ESPN's fine *Outside the Lines* series, the closest thing we have to a *60 Minutes* of sports. Even when you don't agree with Gumbel—he is someone who likes to take drive-by shots at sports, and isn't nearly as in touch with modern sports or modern athletes as he'd like to think he is—at least he is saying something.

But in this case, he cuts athletes too much slack on the basis of color. Because the idea that any athlete can make an asshole of himself as some sort of cultural imperative—that we the White Media are supposed to be more tolerant of asshole behavior because of this "social gulf" Mr. Gumbel talks about—is nonsense. It is nonsense dressed up very nicely in politically correct language. But nonsense.

A load that won't fly no matter how hard Mr. Gumbel tries to give it wings.

Deion Sanders strutting down the sideline in a football game with one hand on the football and one hand behind his head, a flamenco dancer without a fan—this is a black thing? Come on. All the members of that Dream Team at the World Championships of 1994, all that crotch-grabbing that we've already talked about in this book—that was some sort of cultural statement?

Give me a break.

The social gulf that should most concern Bryant Gumbel and all of us who are around sports is not between the playing field and the press box. It is the gulf between the playing field and the stands. In Gumbel's commentary on *Real Sports*, he was leveling a vague charge of racism against the media. Right idea, wrong part of the arena. If there is a real problem with race in sports, it is this.

White audience in the arena most of the time, black stars.

Like the white people with money who used to go up and watch the best singing and dancing in this world at the Cotton Club.

• • •

More and more, you look around at the crowd in a football stadium or a basketball arena or a baseball park, and all you see, rows and rows all the way to the top, are white faces. You look at the crowd at Madison Square Garden sometimes for a Knicks game and feel as if you are looking at the crowd for a New York Rangers hockey game. In the NHL, there is one black player of note, Grant Fuhr of the St. Louis Blues. In basketball, practically all players of note are black.

Every year, Richard E. Lapchick's Center for the Study of Sport and Society, out of Northeastern University, issues what it calls its racial report card. In 1995, Lapchick found that 82 percent of the players in the NBA were black, 68 percent of the players in the National Football League, and 38 percent of the players in major league baseball were either black or Hispanic. This at a time when 12 percent of the general population in this country is black. Lapchick's conclusion, and a proper one, is that sports does offer a tremendous opportunity for minorities.

It does not offer the same sort of opportunities for the ticket-buying public, however. In the end, there is no way of breaking down what percentage of the in-person audience is white. I just go by what I see, twenty years of doing this for a living. And what I see is a white audience. Watching black athletes.

It is a problem that runs more deeply than what Bryant Gumbel considers the lack of sensitivity from white journalists about some black athlete playing hey-look-at-me after a moment of brilliance on the field of play.

A quick story:

In the fall of 1995, the New York Giants retired Phil Simms's jersey in a halftime ceremony at Giants Stadium. It was an emotional night. And the most emotional moment came at the end, when Simms announced to the crowd that he wanted to throw one more pass at Giants Stadium.

And, he said, it would be only fitting if he could throw it to his old friend, and teammate, Lawrence Taylor.

So Taylor took off down the field, and Simms threw the ball long and true, and Taylor caught it. If there can be such a thing as a moment of both clarity and beauty in sports, here was one that had nothing to do with the game being played that night between the Giants and the Cowboys. Here was sports at its best: memory and imagination, and the love that these two men, Simms and Taylor, had for each other. Their memories combined with the memories of the 77,000 people on their feet and cheering everything the two of them had ever been on a Sunday afternoon on that same field.

When it was over, Simms and Taylor embraced, and that crowd went mad for them one more time.

A week later, I got a letter from a Giants fan. He asked in the letter that I not reprint his letter in the newspaper, and asked that his name not be used. I honor both requests here. But this was a thoughtful letter from a thoughtful man about the people who watch sports in this country and the people who attend Giants games in particular. I don't think I am sandbagging the writer by using the last portion of his letter here:

"It is the hypocrisy of these people that I found most interesting. Here they were, standing in front of their seats, some of them nearly weeping with the emotion of the occasion. And they were cheering Taylor, the black player, as much as they were cheering Phil Simms. Then they got into their cars and drove back to their homes in the suburbs. And I guarantee that a few hours after this ceremony, if any of these people had looked out their windows at two o'clock in the morning and seen Lawrence Taylor, or someone looking like him, walking down their street, into their neighborhood, they would have called the police."

White fans want these people to behave, goddammit.

After they've done singing and dancing up a storm.

Glenn (Doc) Rivers comes out of the Maywood section of Chicago, attended Marquette, has played with the Atlanta Hawks, Los Angeles Clippers, New York Knicks, San Antonio Spurs. He goes into television now, he has been successful in the restaurant business, I still believe he will be a successful coach or general manager in the NBA someday. And when talking about white audiences, black stars, he says, "I just worry sometimes that there are still some people up in the stands wondering how it came to be that the slaves get to make $30 million now."

Rivers continues, "Seriously, I believe there are a lot of fans, too many fans, white fans, who look at sports and will never believe, deep down in their hearts, that Doc Gooden, or Doc Rivers, is worth what he is being paid. And you have to believe that some of that is racial."

So the (white) fans will pay money to watch the games, more and more dominated by black athletes. They will root for black athletes to win the game, and they will buy the sneakers and the jerseys and all the other goodies endorsed by these athletes. They will stand in the lines and wait to get the autographs. If there is one way in which sports has improved, and improved dramatically, in the last ten or fifteen years, it is in the endorsement opportunities for black athletes.

Charles Grantham, former head of the NBA Players Association: "The acceptance levels have improved. There was a time when Julius Erving was the only acceptable black athlete to have a relationship with corporate America."

But Doc Rivers is right. Some of the anger fans feel toward Big Sports, and its stars, is racial in nature. It is a shame, but it is also a reality. So much of the other fan anger is justified, a good healthy righteous heat. They get screwed over, over and over again. And again, they are getting screwed over as they are spending more time, and more money, watching sports, than ever before. But some of the anger has nothing to do with sports and everything to do with a distrust—a social gulf—between whites and blacks as deep and powerful as any facet of American life. There is an anger in the stands that can only be explained this way, every time another black athlete does step out of line:

I am not paying *him* to act like *that.*

Whether it is Rodman head-butting the ref, or getting himself ejected from a playoff game between the Knicks and Bulls in the second round of the 1996 playoffs, and taking his shirt off and tossing it into the crowd in a World Wrestling Federation exit from the game, and from the court at the United Center.

Or Mahmoud Abdul-Rauf of the Denver Nuggets refusing to stand for the national anthem.

Or Deion down the sidelines.

The white fan with money in his pocket, wanting his sports but wanting his sports to be a certain way—which means the way it was when he was growing up, before there was all this bullshit from the players, white or black—becomes more and more irritated.

Because *they* don't know their place.

White guys with money pissed off about black guys with money.

Is that beautiful, or what?

SO WHAT DO WE DO?

"I'm not sure we're ever going to change white audiences in sports," Doc Rivers says. "The only times in my career I remember looking up at the crowd and seeing a lot of black faces, I mean a lot, was in Philadelphia in the early '80s, when they had Moses Malone and Julius [Erving]. And the early days of the Showtime Lakers, with Magic and Kareem and James Worthy and Norm Nixon. Before it became cool and hip in Los Angeles to go see the Lakers, and then the audience got rich and white all over again.

"But," Rivers says, "the one thing we've got to do is somehow get kids back inside the arenas. Not just buying the sneakers and the stuff. But going to the games."

There you go. We can't change the last 200 years, but maybe we can open up the doors and windows of sports a little bit. No one is suggesting that only whites can afford tickets to sports events, or that only whites in this country walk around with money in their pockets to burn on sports.

Still, someone like Leigh Steinberg is right when he says that we are forcing more and more middle-class fans away from the park, more of those median families earning $37,000 a year. All you have to do is look around at what it costs to go to a ballgame these days.

Any ballgame.

Anywhere.

Two years ago, the average cost for two people to go to a Houston Rockets game, including tickets, parking, a hot dog, and a soda, was $63.22.

For the New York Knicks it was $108.32.

And $88.32 in New England and $67.48 for Marge Schott's Cincinnati Reds and $64.76 for the Packers.

So it is $125 for a family of four in Houston to see the Rockets and $216 for a family of four in New York to go see a Knicks game.

We have to stop the insanity somewhere. Even if it costs the owners some money. Just because they can get top dollar, for every seat in the house, doesn't mean they have to get top dollar. Or are even entitled to get top dollar. If the owners themselves can't see this, it is the job of a good commissioner to make them see it.

My idea?

That there be a cheap-seat section of every major arena, every ballpark, every football stadium operating in professional sports. Not bad seats. Not nosebleed seats. Cheap seats. That means reasonably priced. Geared toward attracting minorities, geared toward attracting kids. Seats that might not necessarily be filled with anger.

Pie in the sky?

Maybe.

But it is worth a try, before we grow a whole new generation of kids, kids of color, kids without money, who never get a chance to see Michael Jordan in person. Whose total relationship with Jordan, and all like them, will come from television.

Who will grow up thinking their relationship to Jordan and other sports stars revolves around buying Stuff.

So give them a chance to go to the game, every night.

Here is how:

Follow the lead of a Broadway show that opened in 1996 called *Rent.* It is a wonderful hip musical and became a runaway hit, and the producers decided that the way to keep it a hit, because of its subject matter about a new generation of young Bohemians in the '90s, was to attract '90s Bohemians. So the producers held back two choice rows of seats—front-row seats—for every performance. They sold tickets the day of the performance. And young people waited in line to get them the way young people will wait in line to get rock-and-roll concert tickets. Broadway prices had gone through the roof, the way sports prices had gone through the roof. Just not with these tickets.

Twenty bucks.

Not eighty bucks or a hundred bucks, or whatever ticket brokers will charge you for a hit like *Rent.*

Twenty bucks.

Start doing it in sports. At a place like Madison Square Garden, take most of the choice seats, the ones owned by the corporations and the fat cats, and raise those prices. But take 1,000 or 2,000—hey, I've said I'm willing to negotiate on this stuff—and make those $10 tickets. Put them all under the basket if you want to. But get the kids in there. Target kids and inner-city kids especially, the way the dog-ass sneaker companies do with sneakers that the kids can't afford.

Sell them at schools. Move the program from school to school during the season. Give kids sometime at P.S. 93, or whatever, a chance to save up and get one night in the place that has always been billed as the world's most famous arena.

If you put some of the tickets on sale the day of the game, have the ticket windows open as close to game time as possible, as a way of getting the slimy scalpers and the equally slimy ticket brokers out of play.

I know, I know.

The stands are never going to be a beautiful and diverse mosaic. The inside of a ballpark for sports action is never going to look like the inside of a movie theater—all ticket prices the same, everybody equal, first come first served. But we have to take steps at least to try. We have to get kids, and especially kids of color, watching ballplayers of color, heroes of color, on the inside.

I don't want the NBA running "I Love This Game" commercials with mugging, on-the-make celebrities. I want them to do it with kids.

I have had some great days in my life inside baseball parks. I saw Reggie Jackson hit three home runs in the World Series once, and saw Bucky Dent beat the Red Sox with a home run into the left-field screen at Fenway Park on October 2, 1978. I saw Kirk Gibson's World Series home run against Dennis Eckersley in person, and saw Joe Carter end a World Series with a home run at SkyDome off Mitch Williams of the Phillies. I was there when a Mookie Wilson slow roller went right through Bill Buckner's legs at Shea Stadium one October night in 1986. To use a baseball word, I have had my innings. But the best day I ever had at the ballpark was August 12, 1994.

It happened to be the day the baseball players began the most damaging job action in the history of the sport, one that inflicted wounds on baseball that will never heal. Even now, the players union is still trying to put a noble spin on that. Garbage. It was about money and power for them, the same as it was about money and power for the owners. By that date in baseball history, you couldn't tell any of the bastards apart.

We've gone over all that.

I didn't really know what kind of column I planned to write for the newspaper. I just felt that the season would be over by the end of play that day, that the two sides were so far apart that there could be no resolution by September, or even October. I wasn't sure they would all blow off a World Series for the first time, but I sure knew it was a distinct possibility. So I went to Yankee Stadium feeling in my bones that this was the last baseball I would see for a long time.

And when I got there, I saw a ton of kids playing soccer at Joseph J. Yancey Jr. Field, next to Babe Ruth Field, right across the street from Yankee Stadium. The kids were from the Morrisania Air Rights Community Center, between 159th and 160th streets in the Bronx. There were about thirty kids in all, under the supervision of a big, happy, smiling woman named Shirley Marshall. They were all neighborhood kids, and I was willing to bet most of them had never been inside Yankee Stadium in their lives. As if it were some sort of off-limits sports shrine.

Inside the ballpark, grown men making millions were about to throw away the best part of one of the summers with which they have been blessed. They were voluntarily walking out of the ballpark in which they made their living. Across the street were kids who had never been inside.

I decided I was going to take them to a ballgame.

I told Shirley Marshall about my plan.

"How many can go?" she said.

"All of them."

She turned around and yelled, "Who wants to go to a Yankee game?"

The cheer from outside the park that day would be bigger and better than anybody would hear inside.

I ran back across the street and asked one of the guys working the gate which ticket window would be best to buy thirty tickets to the game.

The guy said, “What do you need thirty for?”

I told him.

He said, “Wait right here.” He walked off and talked to his boss, who talked to another boss.

The guy came back to the gate with thirty tickets.

I thanked him.

He said, “We oughta do more of this. Go get the kids and line ’em up and bring ’em right through here.”

So there we were, in formation, all of us from the Joseph J. Yancey Jr. Field, Shirley Marshall in the lead, her assistant Luis Poveda right behind her, me behind Poveda, and then the kids. It was too good to be true on this day, but as we crossed 161st Street in the Bronx, a fourteen-year-old girl named Jackie began to lead them all in “Take Me Out to the Ballgame.”

Most of the kids were of color. All were from the neighborhood. Most were walking through these gates for the first time. We got to our seats just in time for the top of the first. A thirteen-year-old named Eric Cruz, about to become an eighth-grader at the Dr. Roland and Patterson Community Intermediate School in the Bronx, pointed out to where Paul O’Neill stood for the Yankees in right field.

“Babe Ruth played in this ballpark, right?” he said.

I told him, “That’s why they call this The House That Ruth Built.”

“But it was this Yankee Stadium, right? He didn’t play with the Yankees in the other place?”

I said, “The Polo Grounds? No, he was with the Yankees when they built this place.”

“Then they fixed it up about twenty years ago, right?” Eric Cruz said.

"They did."

The kid said, "So Babe Ruth was in the that same spot right there where Paul O'Neill is?"

"The same spot."

The boy smiled and said, "How great is that?"

I asked Cruz, who lived over near Roberto Clemente State Park in the Bronx, if he had ever seen the inside of Yankee Stadium before.

"I just see it when I pass by on the subway train," Cruz said, referring to the 4 train that goes right past the ballpark. "There's this one opening. You have to look fast, but I try to see the ballgame inside every time."

Later that day, Shirley Marshall said, "Kids like these should spend more time in places like this."

I didn't do anything heroic with the kids from the Morrisania Air Rights Community Center. I had passed that same field a hundred times on my way into Yankee Stadium, and always had the same power to get these kids, or kids like them, inside. I'd never thought of it before. So believe me, I'm not looking for a medal.

But I'll tell you what I did do that day:

I made some baseball fans

Again: Sometimes all you have to do is open the doors.

Chapter
Fifteen

SPORTS GERBILISM

The media would love to be part of the solution in sports. It's just that we're too busy being part of the problem.

True Story:

Dick Schaap went to Detroit a couple of years ago to do a feature on the Tigers for ABC. Sparky Anderson was still the manager and the Tigers, at the time, were a surprise team in baseball. One of Anderson's stars was a tough and versatile leadoff man named Tony Phillips.

Schaap went to Detroit with a crew, went over to Phillips and introduced himself, told him what he was there for, asked if he could have a few minutes of Tony Phillips's time.

Phillips did not thank Schaap for giving him a chance to get some network exposure.

Instead Phillips started chewing Schaap out.

The point of his profane outburst was this: Where was Schaap during the rest of his career?

Schaap said, "Excuse me?"

Phillips said, "You're like the rest of the front-runners, coming around now that I'm going good."

Schaap happened to have a Tigers media guide with him. He opened it up, flipped through it until he got to the page with Phillips's lifetime stats on it, and said, "You wanted me to come around when you were hitting .203?"

"Fuck you," Phillips said.

It was one of the most touching scenes between a media person and an athlete since they used to ride the trains together in the old days, don't you think?

Something like it happens every day in a locker room or clubhouse in the United States or Canada.

Athletes hate the media.

The media hates them more.

You're wondering why nobody has much time to talk about your problems?

Hey, we're very busy.

So if you're waiting for us—us being the media, any kind of media—to come riding in to save you from the greedy players and the owner scum, our faces all painted up like Mel Gibson's in *Braveheart*, it's going to be a bit of a wait.

By the way, a digression here: Tony Phillips, with the White Sox by the 1996 season, would be back in the news. He was playing a game in Milwaukee, and some jerk in the stands was showering him with all manner of invective, racial and otherwise. And finally Phillips had enough. He challenged the man to come down under the stands and meet him.

Athletes in all sports have done things like this in the past.

Rarely have they done it while the game was going on.

Phillips did.

He met the guy under the stands, punched his lights out, and went back to his day job with the White Sox. The guy pressed charges, and they both ended up getting fined.

No one is defending the sort of garbage fans think they can get away with now if they buy a ticket. My position on this is clear: You want to be mad as hell about sports, I'm right there with you. You think your ticket entitles you to say unspeakably rude and hateful and vulgar things? You're on your own, pal.

But this was another example of a ballplayer getting dissed, this time by some pig in the stands, and his response—in the moment—being the only thing in the world that mattered. Even if he got hurt, had to leave the game, and his team lost. Schaap couldn't dis Tony Phillips. By God, no one could.

Everything you really needed to know about where the modern sports media is in the 1990s—other than the fact that *Entertainment Tonight*'s Julie Moran once was the great Jim McKay's replacement on *Wide World of Sports*—was on display at Lillehammer's Winter Olympics in 1994. It was like some college course that the whole world was allowed to audit.

(What, you can't envision Julie Moran anchoring the Israeli massacre at the '72 Munich Olympics the way McKay did?)

That was the Olympics of Nancy Kerrigan and Tonya Harding. If you don't remember the story, you spent the months leading up to Lillehammer in the next shack over from the Unabomber's. Because the story was too good—or bad—to be true. Harding and her husband du jour were involved with some goons who whacked out Kerrigan's knee at the United States national championships. They got caught, Kerrigan eventually got better and was able to skate in the Olympics, and the whole thing became one of the biggest and silliest stories ever. It really was as if Neil O'Donnell had hired someone to break Troy Aikman's right arm a month before a Super Bowl game. The fact that all of the stars on Harding's side of the story were dumber than artificial turf made the story even better.

On the other side, of course, you had Kerrigan as America's Skating Sweetheart, even though she would soon be outed as having an affair with her separated—but still quite married—agent, Jerry Solomon.

There you have it, the whole thing was something out of the Harlequin Romance series.

And these two young skaters, in the eyes of the world media, became the 1994 Winter Olympics. Two figure skaters got more coverage than Ali and Frazier got for all three of their fights combined. It was ferret journalism—or Sports Gerbilism, as I like to think of it—of the highest order. Every day, hundreds of camera crews and hundreds of print and television and radio reporters thrown together in a ferret cage—the practice skating rink in a town called Hamar—to get pictures of Kerrigan and Harding skating, and whatever sound bites and quotes they could, all of this in the days before the two of them would skate in the Olympics.

(I didn't cover those Winter Olympics. But if I had, I would have been right there in Hamar with everybody else. There are times in the job when we all should wear T-shirts: Will Whore for Headlines.)

There were some other wonderful stories in Lillehammer, to be sure. Dan Jansen would finally get his elusive Olympic gold medal, after all the years of trying, after all his own Olympic soap operas. Bonnie Blair would certify herself as one of the greatest Olympic athletes we have ever produced in this country; even as a speed skater, a sport only watched at the Olympics, Blair had made herself into a symbol of most of the things we still think are pretty good about sports.

Meaning, she had somehow become a champion in sports without running into, well, Tonya Harding.

And you had Johann Olav Koss and Bjorn Daehlie and Vegard Ulvang, and if you don't know these names, don't feel bad about yourself, neither did most of the Olympic audience when the whole thing was over, because Koss and Daehlie and Ulvang weren't named . . . NANCY AND TONYA!

The first night of the women's figure skating at Lillehammer became one of the most watched televised sporting events in history. From the moment Kerrigan got hit in Detroit and screamed out "Why me?" there hadn't been a day that had gone by without this story being front and center in the sports pages, on the nightly sportscasts, and leading off every *Hard Copy* and A *Current Affair*. There is the ongoing deceit that the Olympics, despite the way the Olympic movement is for sale the way everything else in sports is for sale, is the last refuge of real sportsmanship, real virtue, in sports. That the Olympics produces Real Sports Heroes. And sometimes, in the case of someone like Bonnie Blair, it sure does.

The rest of the '94 Olympics was just the undercard to the Kerrigan–Harding fight. It wasn't just the rabble from tabloid newspapers and tabloid television covering it this way. The most prestigious network news divisions we have were doing the exact same thing.

And when those Olympics were over, the media went back to scratching its collective head, in and out of sports, and saying, "Why don't people care about real news?"

Why?

The answer is so easy even Tonya Harding or one of her goon bodyguards could have understood it.

Because we in the media have trained those people not to care, that's why.

We feed them so much crap, not just about Tonya Harding but about Dennis Rodman, that the crap becomes the real news after a while.

Dennis Rodman shows up at a book signing in Chicago during the NBA playoffs, and Rodman is on a motorcycle and he is wearing more makeup and eye shadow than Elizabeth Taylor at high tide. All in all, he looks like the star of *Priscilla, Queen of the Desert*, just a little taller. This is sports as freak show, the geeking of sports, and it is treated as the only thing happening in Chicago on this day. Rodman is covered on the front pages of both Chicago newspapers, the *Tribune* and the *Sun-Times*. Before Long, Rodman's book, *Bad as I Wanna Be*, is No. 1 on the best-seller list, and his marketing agent is on television bragging about how Rodman's endorsement opportunities went up after he head-butted that referee.

I frankly couldn't understand why Rodman felt he needed a marketing agent.

He's got us.

He's got the sports section marketing his (bare) ass, the same one he shows off on the back of his book. (Another author saving the best side of himself for the end.) He's got television doing the same thing for him. He's in drag on *Sports Illustrated*'s cover long before he shows up at his book signing that way. Why? Because *Sports Illustrated* thinks that Rodman in women's clothing, Rodman in a dog collar, will sell its magazine. It's not the swimsuit issue, but hey, they do the best they can the rest of the year. This is the same year when *Sports Illustrated* runs a cover story about how bad boys and big babies are ruining the NBA.

But pimping for Rodman is aces, right?

Why does Rodman think that he can get away with any manner of outrageous behavior, that he can say anything? Because we keep telling him he can. Because we keep clearing the stage for him, whenever he wants the stage. And he wants it more and more. We keep giving him the microphone and the stage and telling him to let 'er rip. Take it all off. Rodman can live with the shots that people take at him, dismiss them like a glancing elbow under the basket, because that's not the point, the point is being different, bad as he wants to be, different and bad and in play. The only thing he doesn't want is to be ignored. And he is never, ever ignored. He won a playoff game against the Knicks in the spring of 1996 with a couple of wonderful passes; Rodman saved the Bulls that day the way Michael Jordan saves them all the time. After the game, he sat on the court at Madison Square Garden with some sort of big fur hat on his head, shirtless, wearing sunglasses, and in that moment, he was the king of sports again.

The media crowd hung on every word.

The week before, he had been the subject of one of those long "Sunday Night Conversations" on ESPN's *SportsCenter.* Rodman had nothing to say, as usual. It didn't matter. What mattered was that ESPN had him for the sitdown. We had worked our way to this on television from Howard Cosell talking to Muhammad Ali in the old days about Ali's refusal to enter the draft because of religious grounds.

Over all the years, and all the athletes who have tried to be knockoff Alis, just without the charm or the wit, we have worked our way down to bottom-feeding with the likes of Rodman.

And, believe me, it wasn't just ESPN. *Dateline* on NBC ran a Rodman feature. Chris Wallace did a feature on the Bulls for *Prime Time Live.* I like Stone Phillips, who did the *Dateline* piece, very much. Chris Wallace, too. Both did everything with Rodman except start picking out furniture.

Rodman, who has a big best-selling book because he is willing to write about his lurid version of having oral sex with Madonna.

But *Dateline* and *Prime Time Live* do Rodman—boy oh boy, do they *do* Rodman—for the same reason that Connie Chung did Tonya Harding back in 1994.

Give the people what they want, and they'll show up for it.

Why should we worry about the fans' problems—stadium hustles, ticket prices, teams bailing out on them, politicians in bed with owners and everybody in bed with the networks—when we can tell you about Madonna wanting Rodman to be the father of her children?

And you know what those scenes in Lillehammer really were?

They were just good old-fashioned made-in-the-USA Super Bowl coverage coming to the Olympics.

This one time, with this one Nancy–Tonya story, the Olympics were covered the way every single Super Bowl is covered. The Super Bowl being the home office for Sports Gerbilism. You want to know how coverage of sports in this country has dumbed down? Get yourself a press pass and cover any Super Bowl. Where thousands of reporters travel on the same buses for days leading up to the game, talk to the same football players . . . and nothing ever happens.

At least with Nancy and Tonya, bless their hearts, you had the original and rather shocking news story. At the Super Bowl, you have endless questions and endless answers once everybody gets to the host city on the Monday before the game, everybody speculating about a game that usually turns out to be a bigger disappointment than Dennis Rodman's prose. You have the top sportswriters in the country, the network morning shows, the evening news shows, all in one place, millions of words being written, hundreds of miles of tape being used.

About absolutely nothing.

Happens the last week of January, every January.

It's the Bermuda Triangle of journalism.

Every once in a while, you get some real action, as some football player from some team tries to seize the stage and turn himself into a Rodman for a week. Deion Sanders, in particular, is made for

Super Bowl Week, whether he is playing for the 49ers or the Cowboys. He gets to talk as much as he wants, and people have to listen. For him, it's like some media massage parlor. Same with Jerry Jones, the Cowboys' owner. I stood next to him at a conference room at the Cowboys' hotel at Super Bowl XXX, and didn't care too much about what Jones was saying, because I was more interested in the average length of his answers.

It didn't matter whether I was asking the question or somebody else was.

It frankly didn't matter what question Jones had been asked.

His average answer was approximately four minutes and thirty seconds long.

By the end of that particular session, the only relevant question for Jones would have been this one:

"Jerry, you ever find yourself running out of saliva?"

The real game is no longer journalism anymore—not in newspapers, certainly not on television. NBC, for example, has so much money tied up in rights fees, for pro basketball and pro football and baseball and the Olympics, billions of dollars into the next century, that their coverage of a particular sport has become little more than an infomercial for that sport. It doesn't mean they don't have some fine people talking about sports; Bob Costas, who hosts NBC's pregame basketball show and is the network's Olympic host, is one of the great sports broadcasters for this television era, any television era. But there is as much a chance of NBC rocking the boat, considering its investment in these sports, as there is of *Dateline* or Tom Brokaw's news show roughing up the cast of *Seinfeld* or *Friends*.

We saw it a couple of years ago when there were all the stories circulating about Michael Jordan's gambling problems. First there was a piece in *The New York Times* about how Jordan had been seen in Atlantic City gambling the night before a playoff game between the Bulls and the Knicks in New York City. Later came all the allegations from someone named Richard Esquinas about how Jordan had lost as much as a million dollars to him on the golf course.

Esquinas was as oily as most informers.

At the same time, his allegations about Jordan sounded quite plausible.

Jordan wanted those allegations to go away. NBC wanted them to go away, because the NBA playoffs are a hit show and Jordan is the star of that show. He is Jerry Seinfeld of *Seinfeld.* Not just in the playoffs, but anytime he is on television. It's just that in the playoffs the stakes are higher.

David Stern, the NBA commissioner, certainly wanted these charges to go away. Paul Tagliabue, the NFL commissioner, has that phobia about courtrooms and judges we talked about before. It is nothing compared to the fear any sports commissioner has when the word *gambling* gets into the arena. There is one thing that separates the NBA and the NFL and baseball and all the rest of it from professional wrestling: The people know that what they are watching is real.

No one was suggesting for a minute that Jordan, whether he had a serious gambling problem or not, would ever do anything to alter a game. That wasn't the conversation. But it didn't stop people from speculating about what could happen if someone not as rich as Jordan could lose the kind of money about which Esquinas was talking and maybe figure out some creative ways to get out from under.

Stern wanted that sort of talk around his playoffs about as much as he wanted a rat in his Park Avenue office.

(There would even be the rumor later, a big strong rumor, that when Jordan retired from the NBA and went off to play baseball, he was doing that because Stern was prepared to suspend him for a year because of his gambling. Jordan denies it. Last summer, I asked Stern if the story was true. He said it absolutely was not. "It's insulting to Michael and it's insulting to me," Stern said. "Let me ask you something: If you're going to suspend someone for doing something wrong, why would you want to keep that suspension a secret?"

"Because it was Michael Jordan, the greatest ballplayer in history," I said.

"Pete Rose had more hits than anybody in history," Stern said. "The thing never happened."

How did NBC cover the story, ultimately?

By allowing Jordan to be interviewed by Ahmad Rashad, one of his best friends in the world.

Let's just say it wasn't exactly one of those ambush pieces Chris Wallace's dad Mike use to do on *60 Minutes.*

Costas wanted the interview. Jordan "preferred" Rashad. Wouldn't you? NBC rolled over like a puppy. Rashad did the interview. He was the one throwing the batting-practice fastballs. Jordan was the one in sunglasses, preparing for his short-lived career as a minor league baseball player by spraying the ball to all fields.

Rashad asked if Jordan had a gambling problem.

Jordan said no.

My recollection is they talked about the weather after that.

Mainstream journalism, networks sports division, 1990s.

There is the wonderful scene in the movie *A Few Good Men* when Tom Cruise, nostrils flaring, shouts at Jack Nicholson's nut-job Marine, "I want the truth!"

And Nicholson shouts back, "You can't handle the truth!"

The networks cover sports roughly the same way. It is why almost all sports coverage is presented by NBC and ABC and CBS and ESPN as one extended infomercial. If you read the newspapers, you will often see network sports executives talking about how important it is to tell a story to the viewer, the importance of writing and reporting. Then they turn around and hire Julie Moran to host

Wide World of Sports and let Ahmad do Michael when the heat is on Michael. It would be like making afternoon talk-show hosts reporters at the Democratic National Convention. Even hard-nosed newspaper reporters and columnists known as "Information Guys" are more and more hired by the networks to be gossip columnists.

Only in sports television, where the object of the game—or so you would think—would be informing people as well as entertaining them, do you have to put on extra people, create extra jobs, for information.

There are the two series on television I mentioned—*Outside the Lines* on ESPN and *Real Sports* on HBO—that consistently deal with serious issues in sports. The rest of the time, it is guys calling the game and people turning football pregame shows into some sports version of *Hee Haw*, Terry Bradshaw yukking it up with Howie Long and James Brown. Before *Outside the Lines* and *Real Sports*, the last time television had actively tried sports journalism was with the fine Howard Cosell program *Sportsbeat* back in the 1980s. The show was praised for content, never got any ratings, and finally disappeared. It was Cosell's last real television job. Cosell was as bitter at the failure of *Sportsbeat*, the way people did not seem to care about the stories it did or the issues it raised, as he was about anything that ever happened to him, and that is saying a lot. Because he spent the last decade of his life being bitter about just about everything except his family.

I may not agree with what Bryant Gumbel said about white media and black athletes on *Real Sports*, but at least Gumbel was saying something. And maybe HBO is a little freer with its opinions because it is really only in two partnerships: It does boxing regularly, and it does Wimbledon tennis. HBO doesn't have to worry about pissing people off the way, say, NBC does.

And what television does in sports at this time, even more than the sports section, is create a safe house for the athletes. Not everybody is like this. Costas, for example, has been very rough on Rodman over the years, hammered away at both baseball's union and baseball's owners for the damage they have done to the sport. Costas went to Cleveland at the end of the 1995 football season, with the Browns on the way out, and did a commentary about what Modell had done that was both powerful and elegant; it would have run just fine as a column on the op-ed page of *The New York Times*. But as good as Costas is, he knows he is not sitting in the power seat to be jerking the wheel of the boat. He can throw a punch now and again, but is smart enough to know he has to pick his spots. In the old days, Cosell never did. Whether you loved him or not, even if you were sickened by all the meanness he showed at the end of his career—meanness toward me and just about everybody else—you at least knew he was in the room. He had a Foghorn Leghorn voice and you better believe he had opinions, about everything. Only Costas has that kind of voice now at the network level. At ESPN, Keith Olbermann, across the course of an hour-long *SportsCenter*, manages to sprinkle his presentation of the day's sports news with opinion both funny and smartass and informed.

You want to know how scared network people are that someone like Costas might piss off a commissioner or a star player or an agent? He was originally supposed to be the host of *Real Sports*, not Gumbel. The show had always been designed with Costas in mind. And he had talked about a magazine show like this for as long as I have known him, which is about fifteen years. He had done his *Later* show on NBC, had further distinguished himself as an interviewer on shows like *Dateline*. But Costas felt that sports was ready for its own regular *60 Minutes*, and he was ready to be the host of it.

All systems go.

It never came out at the time, because there was really nothing in it for everybody concerned, but NBC didn't want him to do it.

Not because NBC was afraid of Costas working for another network. Because his bosses were afraid of their own talent. Not just any talent. The number one talent, far and away, in the network's sports division. They knew how much Costas bitched about not getting enough time to do real, sometimes biting, commentary, in his host role at NBC Sports. They knew Costas bitched all the time about having a lot to say about things in sports he didn't like, and not nearly enough time to say them. They absolutely did not want him going over to HBO, with nobody looking over his shoulder, and firing away.

He was out, Gumbel was in.

"I give Dick Ebersol [the head of NBC Sports] credit for honesty when he acknowledges that this is a property-driven business," is all Costas will say now. "We can do great production and occasional forays into journalism, but that's not what network sports is primarily about."

You're just there to watch the games, and the commercials, stupid.

All together, one more time: It's the economy, stupid.

Follow the money.

The sports section isn't much better these days.

In the sports section, we either love the athletes or hate them, with hardly any middle ground. In that way, sportswriters, who hate to think of themselves as fans (and hardly ever think about fans), are exactly like fans.

Can't live with the ballplayers, can't kill them.

There was a time in the old days, before the money got crazy, when the relationship between sportswriters and athletes was pretty good. There was always a social gulf there, even when the writers and the ballplayers were riding those trains together, playing cards together, drinking and chasing women together. If you broke everything down to its essentials, it was still Us against Them. Joe DiMaggio had no tolerance for sportswriters, and would do everything possible to stay away from them after games; I've gotten to know him a bit in the last several years, and have often found myself wondering how DiMaggio would stand up to the suffocating scrutiny of the modern sports media, all the gerbilism, his clubhouse crawling with newspaper guys and radio guys and television guys before and after games. The conclusion I end up with is that DiMaggio, with his mania for privacy, would have ended up like Steve Carlton, and not talked to anybody at all.

Mickey Mantle never won any Good Guy Awards from the people covering the Yankees in the 1950s and 1960s, either. For all the grace Mantle showed in both sobriety and in the face of death, he spent most of his playing career hungover and pissed off.

Still, there was a sense in the old days that if the athlete would cooperate, the newspaperman might be able to help him out with some good publicity. Some good play in the papers might help him with endorsements, or maybe even at contract time. Even when Reggie Jackson was one of the biggest baseball stars going in the 1970s, even when he was making more money in salary than just about everybody else in the game, Jackson went out of his way—when he was in the right mood, anyway—to be both talkative and cooperative with the people covering the Yankees. Steve Wulf, once a baseball writer for *Sports Illustrated,* now the fine sports columnist for *Time,* once told me that Reggie was the only ballplayer he'd ever met who spoke at what Wulf described as "perfect notebook speed."

"No kidding," Wulf said. "He'd get going on a certain subject, get really revved up, but the whole time, his eyes would be watching the notebooks. And if he felt as if people were lagging behind him, he'd slow down, I swear to God. It was like watching somebody downshift."

Graig Nettles, Jackson's teammate with the Yankees and never one of his best friends, once put it this way: "If Reggie felt that a sportswriter was walking past his locker without talking to him, he'd trip him."

Not anymore. If you saw an athlete trip a sportswriter these days, chances are he would be doing it for the sheer fun of it.

If he wasn't spraying bleach, the way Bret Saberhagen did one day in the Mets' clubhouse a few years ago. Or threatening the writer, as Bobby Bonilla did with Bob Klapisch, then with the *New York Daily News*, a few years ago. Or dumping a bucket of ice water on the writer, as relief pitcher Willie Hernandez did to Mitch Albom of the *Detroit Free Press*.

Or the athlete could reach out and touch someone the way Anthony Mason did with me.

When he was a kid with the Mets, Darryl Strawberry threatened to stuff me in a garbage can one time. I asked him why.

"You're writing about my wife," he said. "You stay out of my personal life."

Strawberry was close to me; the garbage can was close to both of us.

I said, "I didn't write about your wife."

Strawberry backed up a little, though not quite as far away from that garbage can as I would have liked.

"You didn't?"

"No," I said, and gave him the name of the columnist at my paper who had.

"Well, stay out of my personal life anyway, you little bastard," he said, and walked away.

And it's not just ballplayers hating writers and writers hating ballplayers. The writers also hate the people doing the screaming on all-sports radio and the people on the radio feel exactly the same way. And everybody hates the television guys, because they generally are the ones making the most money. It is why the clubhouse scene in sports, the locker-room scene, once one of the best parts of The Life, has become like an armed camp. There are more prison-yard faces with the writers than the ballplayers, so many more it's not even close.

"Every once in a while, I'd look around at these long faces on the sportswriters in my office, or walking around the clubhouse, and want to say, 'Do any of you guys like your jobs?'" says Buck Showalter, former manager of the Yankees, now with the expansion Arizona Diamondbacks.

One of the big problems here—surprise!—is money. Athletes' salaries may be on a rocket to the moon, but sportswriters' salaries certainly are not. Sportswriters making $50,000 a year or $60,000 a year or even $70,000 covering ballplayers making $7 million. There was always a gap between what the writers were making and what the players were making, all the way back to Babe Ruth. Now it has become ridiculous, and is growing wider and wider every year. So the money isn't any good in sportswriting, and newspapers don't matter the way they used to when they still exist at all. So writers think they are grossly underpaid while covering people they think are grossly overpaid. It is a situation that does not have the markings of a musical comedy.

Mostly sportswriters hate the fact that when they walk up to a player's locker, a star player's locker, this is the look they get: What can you possibly do for me, asshole?

It shows in the coverage, believe me. In the newspaper business in New York, teams don't just lose big games anymore. "CHOKERS!" the back-page headlines read, time and again. New York City becomes "GAG CITY." One time the *New York Post* had the New York Knicks' logo on its back page, only with "Chokers" where "Knicks" should have been. We all get thrilled with the roar of the crowd. Or the rabble. I have done it myself, plenty of times. Bobby Bonilla, when he was with the Mets, finally complained too much one day—or so I decided—and I wrote a column about him and the back-page cartoon had Bobby Bo in diapers, under the headline "Baby Bo."

Some of the reasons they hate us are very good.

So if you are wondering why nobody is paying attention every single time a fan is getting screwed over, the reason is simple enough: The people you're counting on are worrying too much about how *they're* getting screwed over.

Like I said, keeps us real busy.

And talk radio, even though it seems to provide very good therapy for the people on the phones, hasn't helped anybody very much. Ten years ago there was no such thing as all-sports radio. Now there are forty-two stations across the country. It was all started by a man named Jeff Smulyan with WFAN in New York City. (That station has become one of the great radio success stories of all time. The funny thing is, the station was not built on sports, it was built on the immense popularity of Don Imus's program, now syndicated in eighty-five cities. Imus's show runs on WFAN between 5:30 and 10 every morning and makes more money for Infinity Broadcasting, now the station's parent company, than Infinity's accountants can count. Imus sat down at the microphone, and within a few years, WFAN was the top billing station for ad revenue in the country. It wasn't the calls from Charlie in the Bronx.)

Now the people in sports feel as if they are under attack twenty-four hours a day.

Does nothing to improve ballplayer–athlete relations.

Just makes the coverage feel more like a scorched-earth policy to the ones being covered.

The ballplayers—or coaches, or managers—get into the car after the game or before the game and after a while, because they are drawn to these stations like moths to a flame, they don't distinguish any longer between the caller and the host. They just feel as if they are under siege, all the time. Day or night. In that way, talk radio has dramatically altered the landscape in sports over the last ten years, the way it has altered the landscape in this country. Opinion hasn't become any more informed. But if *SportsCenter* on

ESPN is a way of bringing the sports world together every night at 11 or 11:30, or whenever one of the one million televised college basketball games ends, talk radio also brings sports fans together in this way:

Here is a place where they get to bitch and somebody has to listen. There are no boundaries, other than language. There is no right or wrong. Sometimes it really is impossible to distinguish between the callers and the hosts. But the heat is always turned up. ESPN does an *Outside the Lines* special on talk radio, and here is Peter Brown, a talk-show host out of Chicago—and someone with whom I converse occasionally on ESPN radio—bragging that he can (he believes) get coaches fired.

As if that is a skill now in the sports media, like writing a good lead, or doing the kind of graceful commentaries Jack Whitaker used to do on television for CBS and ABC.

And everybody, callers and listeners, feel as if they have the undivided attention of the people about whom they are bitching.

There's no need to run a radio poll here about whether or not they would rather bitch or have sex.

Bitching would win every time.

SO WHAT DO WE DO?

In this case, "we" means the media.

All of us.

The sports section of the newspaper, my sports section and everybody's else's, should start covering the business of sports, the nuts-and-bolts business, as ferociously as it covers the games. We should do a better job of finding out how much teams are making and how much they are charging, and if teams keep trying to hide the books and hide the numbers, we should go after them the way we go after the players. We need to know how much the owner of the team made last year, from sports and from his other businesses. Every time ticket prices go up, it should be more than a small box buried deep in the sports section; it should be a big story, with responses from the people selling the tickets and the people buying the tickets.

It is routine to refer to Barry Bonds as the Eight-Million-Dollar Man. Because of a balloon payment in Patrick Ewing's contract, a salary cap dodge and nothing else, Ewing was paid $18 million for the 1995–96 season. You could not read a story about Ewing all season long, listen to the radio for a day, without that figure being brought up, by someone. So shine the same sort of light on the finances of the owners. Do it to Steinbrenner and Turner and Marge Schott and the rest of them. Steinbrenner has his deal with the Madison Square Garden television network, one that pays the Yankees nearly $50 million in rights fees. Where does that money go? How is it divided among Steinbrenner's other partners? (John McMullen, at one time a Steinbrenner partner, once said, "There is nothing more limited than being a limited partner of George Steinbrenner's.") If a limited partner wants to sell his share, can I buy it? Can you? The fans have a right to know all of this, and we don't do a nearly good enough job of telling the owners about it.

And every week, there should be a consumer section in the sports section, prominently displayed, in which fan issues are addressed. There should be more feedback from the fans than just shrill voices on the radio. On Sundays, the *New York Daily News* now runs a regular page with a guest columnist, and reader feedback on a particular issue in sports. It's a nice start, but isn't enough. There are all these statistics around, some of them in this book, about how much it costs for a family of two, a family of four, to go to a ballgame. We don't just need to stay on top of that year by year, we need to do it month by month.

How are the ushers treating you at the ballpark?

What kind of service do you get?

When you have a problem, how helpful is ballpark security?

Is it better at the end of the season than at the start?

All under this heading: Do you feel that when you go to the ballpark, you are getting your money's worth?

When you go to Yankee Stadium or Dodger Stadium or Orioles park at Camden Yards, are you treated like a paying customer or are you treated like a field hand?

Too often, I read the newspaper and think that the only thing that matters to sportswriters is acting tough in front of other sportswriters. They're not serving you, they're posing for each other. Same with the people on the radio. As much as they criticize newspapers, they rush to the sports section every morning to start making up their minds about the issues of sports. And the same sportswriters who treat radio hosts with contempt listen to them and try to make up *their* minds about things. (I've always felt that if a story broke at a certain time of day, neither the sportswriters nor the hosts would know what the hell to think. They'd just be waiting for someone else to make the first move.)

Sports Gerbilism. Everyone goes into the cage, runs around for a while, comes out with one opinion. Then they all want to tell *you* what to think, whether they really know or not.

And everybody forgets that this is supposed to be a service business as well as entertainment, and we're supposed to be serving the readers. The fans. Making sure that they're being taken care of. Making sure that they are being served as well as they should be, no matter what a mess we've made of things.

We need more shows like *Real Sports* and *Outside the Lines.* A lot more. Whether they get the biggest ratings, the biggest ad rates, or not. It would be nice to see the people at the networks get off their hands and knees once in a while, so the sponsors can stop paddling their bottoms. It doesn't have to stop with beautiful up-close-and-personal features during the Olympics, no matter how beautiful to look at they are. It doesn't have to be NBC's patriotic coverage of things like the Atlanta Olympics, as if American gold medals are all that matter, American athletes. Every night, NBC wanted the Olympics to be a musical, built around our National Anthem.

In the end, it wouldn't cost the networks all that much money, or time, to show some guts once in a while.

It wouldn't hurt any of us if we did a better job than we've been doing of outing some of these creeps.

Because there is no question that we have let you down.

Chapter Sixteen

SOMEONE TO WATCH OVER YOU

As it happens, Ralph Nader was way ahead of me, and everybody else, about sports, by nearly twenty years.

But then Nader has always been a step or two ahead, even when people have not taken him seriously, or treated him like the nutty professor, or dismissed him as an antique, as though fighting for the consumer has somehow gone out of style. As if something like that can ever go out of style.

All the way back in November of 1977, Nader and Peter Gruenstein formed a group called FANS—The Fight To Advance Nation's Sports.

I think Rodman has had hair colors that lasted longer.

No one cared about FANS at the time. No one took it seriously; I barely remember it. People mostly looked at Nader as some crackpot trying to save a world that didn't need saving. So they ignored him and waited for him to go away. Which he and Gruenstein finally did.

"We found out something when we tried to get into sports," Ralph Nader says now. "They're very turf-oriented. It was like, 'Who the hell are you?' Of course, maybe one of the reasons was that FANS was prepared to take on sportswriters because they were such patsies and sycophants for the owner . . . and they didn't like it."

(Damn right. Hey, we'll decide who the patsies and sycophants are around here.)

But you want to know something? Ralph Nader and Peter Gruenstein sure as hell saw the storm clouds on the horizon. Maybe right behind the first luxury boxes. FANS' stated mission from the start—as published in *Leftfield*, the organization's journal—was simply this: to represent the interests and views of the nation's 100 million sports fans wherever such representation was needed, before leagues and player associations, before individual owners or the broadcast media or Congress, before state and local governments.

They also had this crazy idea that sports should be more fun than it was, even back then.

"Fans are angry," Peter Gruenstein said nineteen years ago. "They are being ripped off and they know it. And we think they want to do something about it."

Fancy that.

FANS was launched with Nader's help in the form of a $10,000 loan. Membership dues were nine dollars a year. "We want to ensure that the average fan can obtain tickets to events," Gruenstein said at the time. "And we want to ensure that fans have meaningful input into proposed policies and rules changes—for example, the designated-hitter rule and interleague play in baseball, the two-point conversion in pro football, and the three-point shot in basketball."

(At the time the journal was written, only the DH rule was in effect.)

The first edition of *Leftfield* also set forth a Bill of Rights for fans, with ten points that can be summarized thusly:

1. Fans should influence rules changes.
2. Fans have a right to know about the operation and practice of organized sports.
3. Fans have the right to purchase reasonably priced tickets and to be treated with courtesy and respect.
4. Tickets should be available to everyone, not just the elites.
5. Fans have the right to see their interests represented before Congress.
6. Fans should have games broadcast the way they want them shown.
7. Fans have the right to have their interests in the resolution of sports disputes effectively expressed.
8. The interest of fans in the integrity of a team should also be effectively expressed.
9. Fans, as average citizens, have the right not to see those in sports treated as if they are above the law.
10. Sports entities that rely on public funds have an obligation to serve the public and disclose relevant information.

I came to Ralph Nader after I'd finished writing this book and asked him for help. I hadn't remembered FANS. I was just another one who'd ignored Nader, and his organization, back in 1977. I didn't get my first copy of *Leftfield* until 1996.

"Where were you when I needed you?" Ralph Nader said.

"It's the other way around now," he was told. "Now we need FANS."

"I've been ready for twenty years," he said.

We can still call it FANS, by the way. Or the National Organization of Sports. The name doesn't matter; the need for advocacy does. It has reached the point where we need someone to call, whether it's because of an usher or ticket taker at the ballpark forgetting who the customers are or the cable guys ripping us off, or owners jacking up prices every time they want to sign a Best Available ballplayer, or the ballplayers themselves acting as if we really were put on this earth to help take care of them.

It has reached the point where we need to make it somebody's job to look out for us.

Full-time job, too.

But we also have to look out for each other.

"The only way for fans to get sports back is through collective action," Ralph Nader says today. "First of all, they've got to get rid of tax subsidies and contracts that are extremely one-sided in favor of sports moguls, and their negotiation with the municipalities is secret. All this should be public. Any decision should be subject to a referendum. Because in the end the taxpayer doesn't get a return for his coerced investment. The percentage of the concessions, the dirt-cheap rent that's charged, if there's any rent charged, the other subsidies, they're all extremely one-way. So the first thing to do is drive it to a referendum, which gets it out of closed rooms. Once you drive it to a referendum, the press has a greater interest in demanding disclosure. There's more debate. The other thing [the press can do] is show callousness, in Maryland, for example, in Baltimore, where they're shelling out $300 to $400 million for a football team while the Baltimore city schools are crumbling. I mean, the schools and the clinics are in horrible shape, and in Roman gladiator circus style, they're shelling out money for sports."

Go, baby.

"There has to be lawsuits," Ralph Nader continues. "One of these days, the Supreme Court is going to rule that, guess what, you can't use tax money to further the profits of sports corporations, that it's not a public purpose. . . . For a variety of reasons, these suits have been squelched in the past. Either they attack the suits or settle out. But this Court we have now is the kind that would take something like this very seriously. Because tax money is supposed to be used for a public purpose, highways and parks and bridges and sewage. They've even expanded it in some state courts to include just creating jobs. I mean, my God, we're talking about $300 million for a stadium in Baltimore, but where else can that money be spent? I'll tell you where. For schools and for clinics."

Three hundred million in Baltimore, maybe as much as a billion to keep George Steinbrenner fat and happy in New York instead of New Jersey. What Nader is talking about here is simple enough:

Good money being thrown after bad-ass owners.

Too much of it our money.

What you have in Nader, then and now, is someone who is not swept away by the romance of sports, the nonsense of sports, who does not want to meet the athletes or glad-hand with the owners. Who comes at this with the same fierce dignity he has come at everything in a public life, with the same clear eyes.

Nader says, "The problem we have now is that you feel as if you have to combine a fans' group with a taxpayers' group. I mean, in the last year, this whole thing has gone totally berserk. There is no shame whatsoever. The owners just paddle around and say, 'All right, Memphis, what do you give?'"

So Nader is finally asked this question: How do we have FANS back, how do we have our National Organization of Sports, and give it some muscle?

"You need at least ten thousand fans at the start who are dues-paying members, at something like twenty-five dollars a year," he says. "For that, you'll probably need about half a million a year in seed money that would help in a lot of ways, to get lists of people and use them to start getting out information.

Nader says it wasn't just sportswriters sandbagging him in 1977, he was also ridiculed by owners. Even George Will (who wrote the adoring *Men at Work* about baseball a few years ago, and still gets aroused just thinking about Cal Ripken making a great play in the hole) wrote a column ridiculing the idea that sports fans in this country needed some watchdog group looking out for them.

Nader: "Will wrote something like, What is this, every time there's a perceived grievance, there has to be a citizens' group?"

Maybe in the end, the need for reform in sports, all over the board, will be swallowed up by our growing addiction for sports, our need for sports, the need of fans—particularly those with money in their pockets—to be on the inside, to run with the crowd. We've already talked about private seat licenses, the wave of the future in sports. And what they really are is just the newest kind of sports drug, at least for the people who can afford them.

Ballpark crack.

The first day that the Carolina Panthers put private seat licenses up for sale, they sold $105 million of them.

One day.

One hundred and five million.

Another side street in sports making you proud to be an American.

When the Rams moved to St. Louis, there were 73,710 applications filed for the 46,000 PSLs.

Thank you, sir, may I have another?

(Don't these people, when they're down there groveling in front of some hair-spray-for-brains like Georgia Frontiere, worry about knee burns? No kidding. Sometimes we should all, as fans, think about endorsing knee pads.)

Nader tried to fight back in 1977 and everybody tried to laugh him out of sports. Now we need someone like him to be in place by 1997. These days, Nader still has his hands full with a job he still describes as Consumer Advocate. Most of his time is spent with the

Center for the Study of Responsive Law in Washington, D.C. Peter Gruenstein is now a lawyer in Anchorage, but would love to get back in the game. And sports fans would be lucky to have him.

So let's get them back in the game. Let's get at least the 10,000 fans Nader and Gruenstein say we need to start. If you are really interested, write Ralph Nader at this address:

FANS
c/o
Center for the Study of Responsive Law
P.O. Box 19637
Washington, D.C. 20036

If we do get to 10,000 or close enough, we will go about the business of putting together an operation. Nader and Gruenstein will be the first two members of the Board of Directors. I'll be a third. The other voices in this book, Doc Rivers and Keith Olbermann and Dave Checketts and Paul Westphal, they're in, too.

And if we do get this thing up to speed, if there are enough fans willing to put up money to fight back, instead of putting it into the pockets of the owners and the players and occasionally the politicians—"By the time the Browns thing was over, the Maryland legislature looked like a house of prostitution," Nader says—then we will need someone to be commissioner.

Commissioners of FANS.

It would have to be someone who is a sports fan himself. It would have to be someone to command the attention and respect of everybody in sports just by showing up for the game.

Don't worry, I've got a guy:

Mario Cuomo.

If there really were such a thing as commissioner of professional sports in this country, if there were a job like that, I'd hire him in a shot. Hell, baseball should have hired him to be commissioner as soon as Cuomo lost his job as governor of New York in 1994. I still wish the country had gotten the chance to hire him as president. He is an old St. John's baseball player, and even gave the minors a shot in the Pirates' system. He would only be perfect. He doesn't agree with everything I say about sports, or everything Ralph Nader does. He sure was on the inside trying to keep the Yankees in New York, even if it did mean building a slob like Steinbrenner a new ballpark. And I don't care. If there is even a chance that fans are willing to organize and start fighting back, Cuomo would be made for that kind of fight. Always, when he talks, people listen.

"I'd be proud to serve," he says.

He would be what we have needed for a long time.

The commissioner of us.

Chapter Seventeen

MAD AS HELL

Sometimes, you just read the papers or watch the news and want to do more than have Ralph Nader on your side, you want to go out and finally organize the Sports Police. You want to deputize all the people who still care, and authorize them to go around and make a citizen's arrest every time somebody goes too far over the line.

Again.

It would have to be a big police force, but believe me, I can supply the manpower. And womanpower.

(The woman won't just carry badges, but pictures of Christian Peter.)

Because the law we have in sports doesn't appear to be enough. At least not enough of the time.

After everything that has happened to Albert Belle and around him, he still doesn't learn, even though his supporters, on the Indians and even in the media, keep telling us what an intelligent, educated man he is. Here is Belle in a June game against the Milwaukee Brewers, running down a little second baseman named Fernando

Vina. Not just running him down, but trying to throw a forearm shiver at Vina's face. Vina was standing in his path between first and second. In this case, the baserunner can legally hit the fielder. It happens all the time. Just not the way Belle did it.

The Players Association, of course, said Belle was innocent. In fact, Gene Orza of the Players Association said that the forearm to the head never happened, that our eyes were playing tricks on us. Orza said that Belle was being unfairly singled out in this case, that he was being punished for his rap sheet. When Orza finished, here is what I told him: "Good."

"Albert doesn't just react," Orza of the Players Association said. "Unfortunately, he overreacts."

It was something we had all been able to figure out on our own.

If you were in Milwaukee that night, you wanted to be an official, deputized member of the Sports Police and just go into the Indians' clubhouse afterward and hand Belle some walking papers and say to him, "You're suspended until you wise up, you jerk. Pack up your stuff and go home and wait for some teenager to ring your doorbell."

I know.

Makes you hot just thinking about it.

Are all athletes out of control? Of course they're not. Of course the good guys will always outnumber the bad guys, by a lot. Good news about their good deeds will never be as racy or thrilling as the news when they misbehave. "Bad is better than good," Curry Kirkpatrick once wrote in *Sports Illustrated,* in a tongue-in-cheek lead to a profile of the young Ilie Nastase. It is the way we seem to cover sports and everything else these days.

Maybe that is why bad seems to be winning. Bad attitudes. Bad values. Even, in Rodman's case, bad hair.

Badasses, more of them than we can ever remember, all over the map.

Thinking they run the world.

Of course, it is not true that all players are rude, greedy bastards. Not all owners have rocks in their heads, and cash registers where their hearts are supposed to be. Not all commissioners, acting as otherwise, hide under the bed at the sign of trouble, or when asked to make tough decisions.

Not all sports fans are mad as hell.

Just way too many.

And just because sports is as addictive as ever doesn't mean it is better than ever, doesn't mean it is as fun as it should be. Or used to be. There is no law ever passed that says sports is supposed to be fun all the time, or some kind of happy fantasyland, the Magic Kingdom with bats and balls and helmets and sticks. I used to caddy for my father when I was a boy, and every once in a while, after he would miss a golf shot into the woods, he would sigh and say, "And your mother thinks I'm having fun."

Sports is never going to be as simple or as uncomplicated as it once seemed. Sports is never going to be 1955, ever again, because the country is never going to be 1955 again.

"This isn't about the 1950s," John Gabriel, the talented young general manager of the Orlando Magic, says. "This is about where we want sports to be in the year 2000. We have to decide what we want."

We want it to be better, that's what. We want to hold on to our players and to our teams, and not have to throw money at the players and the teams to have them stay. Gary Bettman is right: The players aren't lawyers. They sure as hell are not. Lawyers moving from firm to firm don't threaten the legal profession, any more than I've threatened newspapers by bouncing around the past few years. Sports is different. We escape to sports *because* it is different. If allegiance to a team or a player is silly and childish, if the illusion that fans and players can sometimes be in the whole thing together is an illusion, it is still a wonderful illusion. Sports can still be the kind of escape that great literature provides, or great theater, or a great movie.

It is still supposed to be magic.

It is supposed to be the excitement we felt when Magic Johnson made his comeback in January of 1996, not the sadness we felt when he finished the same season with so little grace.

The first sports event I remember watching was the New York Giants–Baltimore Colts sudden-death championship game in 1958, still regarded by many as the greatest football game ever played. We watched it in the living room of my aunt's house on Earl Avenue in Oneida, New York. I was six. My father was there, and three of my uncles. What I know about the game—the facts of it, the big plays–I have really learned in all the years since, all the years of being in this life. In memory, I just remember all the talk in the living room that day about how Unitas was killing us, and then the groans and shouts when Alan Ameche ran into the end zone to win the game for the hated Colts.

"The template was cut" is the way my friend Pete Hamill describes a day like that in sports. "For me it was the first time I saw Jackie Robinson."

More than anything, I remember the magic of the afternoon. Not just because I was in there with the grown-ups, a part of their action. Into the game. I remember the excitement that wouldn't leave me even after Ameche scored. All this time later, I can remember where everybody sat in the room, where the black-and-white set was.

Sports does that.

Sports is the moment, the bright loud moment, but it is as much memory, and imagination. There was a spark for me that day that I would carry with me the rest of my life. The spark for my oldest son was the first trip he made to Madison Square Garden to watch

Michael Jordan play. Jordan had a terrible game. He hurt his ankle. The Knicks killed the Bulls. Jordan left the game for a while because of the ankle and then came back.

My oldest son, the one who dreams of being a point guard in the NBA, remembers everything about the day. Everything. Including Jordan diving for this one loose ball.

Everything about the day was good.

Only more and more, he puts on the television in the morning and sees something lousy. Van Exel. Rodman. Belle going after Fernando Vina. And then at night, he can't watch the biggest games of the year, the championship games of everything except the Super Bowl, which actually starts at a decent hour, because the networks show everything too late. The network guys tell you that the games have to start in the East so they don't blow the audience in the West. Garbage. The reason why NBC, or CBS before them, wants to start World Series games in the East as close to nine o'clock as possible, is that they always want to squeeze one more prime-time show in between eight o'clock and nine. And we just nod our heads and wait for the first pitch like good soldiers, because what are our options?

Call the Sports Police?

Where's the equivalent of a 911 number for that when we really need one?

I still love going to the games. I still walk into the ballpark or the football stadium or the basketball arena sure I am going to see something that night I've never seen before in my life. It is that hope that keeps me coming back. There are times when sports is still something grand and joyful. Here it is a Sunday in June, and late in the day, Tom Watson wins the Jack Nicklaus Memorial golf tournament in Dublin, Ohio. I am a golfer and Watson is one of the great golf champions, but he has not been able to win a tournament in nine years. Nine years. He has had a case of nerves on the putting green that has lasted at least half of that time. Time and again we have watched him come close, only to miss so many short putts down the stretch, sometimes we didn't even want to watch anymore.

Now he wins again, rolling in a birdie putt on the last green that is nine years long, and then walking off the green and hugging Nicklaus, with whom he had battles in golf that will always be discussed. And suddenly it is not the spring of 1996 but the summer of 1977, and Watson is putting an arm around Nicklaus's shoulder after beating him on the last hole of the British Open in Turnberry, Scotland. Watson had shot 65–65 the last two days. Nicklaus had shot 65–66 to lose by a stroke. It was not just golf at its best, but sports at its best.

I was at Turnberry in '77, and all this time later I can tell you everything about the day, right through dinner with Tom and Linda Watson afterward in the huge dining room at the Turnberry Hotel. And late that night, I was coming out of the hotel bar with Dan Jenkins, and there, alone on a dance floor, on the night after Watson had beaten the greatest golfer who ever lived in the greatest British Open ever played, I saw him dance with his wife, while a Scottish band that looked as if it should have been working a wedding played "We'll Meet Again."

Sports will always be able to take us back.

The problem is this: There are just too many times when we are all too willing to go back.

Because we really do believe, with all our hearts, that the old days in sports, even with all the problems of the old days, were better than these. Willie Mays was no sweetheart. Mays could glare you away from his locker, too, from time to time. He didn't routinely tell reporters to screw off, either. I see it all the time. A kid from ESPN went into the Yankees' clubhouse to talk to John Wetteland during the 1995 season. Not only did Wetteland, who didn't know the ESPN kid from the prime minister of Egypt, tell the kid to screw off, he tried to get Wade Boggs not to talk to ESPN, either.

John Franco of the New York Mets, somebody with whom I have always gotten along fine, saves a game at a time when he has been getting booed and makes the famous, um, screw-you salute, one arm across the other. It shows up, as you can imagine, on the back pages of the New York tabloids.

Franco's reaction?

He blames the press for "bad journalism."

Not himself for being a very bad boy.

And you know what? In that moment, Franco was the most honest guy going in sports. He was just saying to fans what athletes want to say all the time. He was saying it in the middle of the field, in front of everybody, for the world to see. You dare come to the ballpark and boo him when he can't get enough people out?

Screw you.

Screw you, who paid for the tickets and the parking and the food and sat in traffic before the game and then sat in traffic again after the game. Screw you, and those kids you might have sitting next to you.

Screw you for coming out to the park and hurting John Franco's feelings.

This is the culture. So is blaming somebody else afterward. It happens all over American life, so we shouldn't be surprised that it happens in sports, except sports was supposed to be more fun than this. John Franco blames the media, so does Leigh Steinberg, and Charlie Grantham, who used to run the players' union in basketball before the players decided another union head could get them more money, before too many of Charlie Grantham's players, ones he had helped make rich, thought he was working too closely with NBA commissioner David Stern.

All of them on the inside say we in the media, we the fans, focus on the money too much.

Sometimes we do, no question.

But another rule of modern sports seems to be this: The players want to make as much money as they can, they keep score with each other on the money, owners can't ever disrespect them by offering too little money, but the rest of us aren't supposed to dwell on the goddamned money.

Another thing that hurts their feelings.

Deion Sanders made television commercials that helped him brag about his new $30 million contract with the Cowboys. At his first press conference in Dallas, he did all sorts of material about the $30 million. Then he threw a fit one day in the middle of the season because the devil media in Dallas is—oh sure, you guessed it—focusing too much on his salary.

Sanders is celebrated in the media for being colorful, and so is Andre Agassi, and at the very same time in sports, which means right now, Pete Sampras, one of the great tennis players of all time, a champion whose professional life has been mostly a model of grace and professionalism, is castigated for being too boring. Good is not nearly as interesting as bad. People long for the past in sports, and then when someone comes along who is of the past, who embodies everything we believe the best sports heroes used to be, we make fun of him, say he is duller than Bob Dole.

"People want to sit there and say, 'I wish I could go back,'" John Gabriel says. "But, let's face it, we're not going back. [Having said that] it doesn't mean we have to give up on our values, or what we believe is the right way to run sports. What we really need to do is take a lot of the way sports used to be, the type of people we used to have in sports, those type people, and concentrate on how to fit some of that in with the way things are now."

Gabriel pauses.

"So how do we bridge the gap between the 1950s and 2000?

How do we bridge that gap? As managers, the only thing we can do is stick to values. We must put the best chemistry on the floor, not just the best players. Good talent dominates this league and every other league, don't get me wrong. But if you put the right chemistry on the floor, you will have success. That group of players will represent you with their statistical achievements, wins and losses. But right next to that, you would want them to represent you in the most positive light off the court."

Gabriel is the man who orchestrated the draft-day trade that brought the Magic Anfernee Hardaway and three No. 1 draft choices, after everyone was sure that Chris Webber would be playing next to Shaquille O'Neal for the next decade or so. At the end of the 1994–95 season, the Magic were in the NBA Finals, and some people thought they would soon be winning the first of four or five titles. Only, they got swept by the Houston Rockets. At the end of the 1995–96 season, they got swept by the Chicago Bulls. And all of a sudden, the league's Team of the Future was saying good-bye to Shaquille O'Neal forever.

Gabriel was finding out what everybody finds out in sports, and that is how fast things change, how little permanence there is.

"If there's one thing we've lost in sports," John Gabriel says, "it's earning the dollar, earning the notoriety. That's sort of gone out the window. The day of the guaranteed contract has sort of set the stage for players to go out and live the lives of those that have been prosperous or successful before they have done anything. And that has probably hurt the game.

"And the thing is," he continues, "I don't know where you point the finger. Is it the fans for paying the dollar to see these guys, is it the ownership for giving the money in advance? You sure as heck can't blame the player for taking the millions we throw at them, particularly in the NBA before we had a rookie salary cap, guys getting forty and fifty million dollars before they even laced up their first NBA shoe. But I think we have an obligation as franchises, I think the NBA has an obligation, to guide these people so that they do not just become the great athletes we're paying them to be, but citizens as well, so that their success off the court can mirror their success on the court. There's nowhere in these contracts these people sign that says they have to be role models. That's up to the individuals, and up to the people who view this sport. But I can tell you that we as a team in Orlando emphasize what we expect from our players off the court as well as on it."

This is a good smart man talking, one who does seem to care about more than just the standings, the bottom line. If he sounds like a dreamer here, that's all right, we need more dreamers just like him. He has tried to do things right in Orlando. O'Neal and Hardaway are two of the most gifted young players to come along in years and years. Gabriel had done a fine job of surrounding them with good role players. The coach of the team, through the 1995–96 season, was a decent man named Brian Hill. And even with all that in place, exceptional talent, good support system in the front office, there was the scene during the season when Shaquille O'Neal, the week after his grandmother died, would not give Hill the courtesy of letting him know whether or not he would show up for a nationally televised game against the Bulls.

There was the night in Detroit when Anthony Bowie, one of those role players, was so obsessed with getting the first triple-double of his career (double figures in points, rebounds, assists) that he called a time-out in the last seconds of a game the Magic were winning by a rout, so that he could get the last assist he needed. Doug Collins, the Pistons' coach, was so upset he basically pulled his players off the court. Hill, instead of sitting Bowie's ass on the bench, said he wanted no part of the whole episode. So the Magic inbounded the ball, Bowie passed to a teammate, the teammate scored, Bowie had his triple-double.

The NBA had a really good shiner the next day, as did John Gabriel's Orlando Magic, an organization where the people still talk about values in sports, still seem to care about them.

Then one of his players goes out and orders up a triple-double of the kind of I-me garbage that keeps trying to ruin everything.

You know the response to this, of course. The People in Charge, the people who run sports at just about every level, look at the attendance, the ratings, the money that keeps pouring in, and they say, "Enough people must like the way things are going."

They shrug and say, "How bad can things be?":

The bottom line is good and the People in Charge don't give a flying, um, falk about how we get there.

But the question all of us who are supposed to love sports should be asking is this one:

"How can we make things better?"

How do we start teaching kids the values about which John Gabriel speaks instead of corrupting them at earlier and earlier ages? Marcus Camby comes out of the projects of North Hartford, Connecticut. He is another young star of sports who somehow made it to school, made it home from the courts, with the sound of gunfire around him, and drugs everywhere. He has a strong mother and a strong support system, and he made it out of North Hartford to a superb college career at the University of Massachusetts. Instead of staying around for his senior year, he decided to enter the NBA draft, assured by most of the experts and pseudo-experts that he had to be one of the first three players chosen. Because of the way the rookie salary cap is now structured in the NBA, Camby was guaranteed a three-year contract worth $9.1 million.

Long way from North Hartford.

The kind of story to make you cheer, the way we once elected Michael Irvin for making it out of his corner of Fort Lauderdale.

Only, on the day before the NBA Finals were about to begin—as Camby was about to participate in a big rookie camp in Rosemont, Illinois, just a few miles from where the Bulls and Sonics would play the Finals—it came out that Camby had been taking money from prospective agents for a couple of years. A few thousand here, a few thousand there, or so he told the *Hartford Courant* newspaper, which got the goods on him.

"I know I did wrong," Marcus Camby tearfully told the *Courant.*

Sometimes they actually admit that in sports. But only when they get caught.

Camby was just another kid who couldn't wait for the real goodies, who got tired of looking around from college basketball at all the money everybody else was making, got legitimately dog-ass tired of that, and put his hand out early. And you want to know why no moral alarm went off for him?

Because there isn't that kind of alarm in sports.

Not anywhere.

I have covered sports, in the newspaper and in magazines and on television and even on the radio (WFAN in New York, for seven months in 1993). I have written books about sports. I started writing for the *Boston Globe* when I was a sophomore at Boston College in the early 1970s, and by the time I was twenty-four I had my own column in the *New York Daily News,* and this is the only life I have ever known, or wanted.

I saw all of Magic Johnson's career and all of Larry Bird's. I have seen all of Jordan. I was at the hockey rink in Lake Placid in 1980 when an extraordinary, unlikely group of American kids shocked the world by upsetting the team from the USSR; it is still the greatest sports event I have ever covered, or expect to cover. I saw Carl Lewis win all his Olympic gold medals, all the way through the long jump competition in Atlanta. I was at Fenway Park in 1978 when the Yankees played the Red Sox in a one-game playoff for the American League East, and I remember standing with Roger Angell of *The New Yorker* at the batting cage that day.

It was October 2, and it was one of those glorious late-summer afternoons in Boston, and this would be the final chapter of one of the great baseball summers.

"This is ridiculously exciting," Angell said.

Mostly I have felt that way about the life.

Only there are these days now, and they come more frequently, too frequently, when I feel as if sports is running me off, and I tell you, if it can happen to me, it can happen to anybody. It is more work than ever to go down to the clubhouse or locker room and listen to the players, when the players are in the mood to talk. It is more work than ever to listen to similar crap in the press box, where original thought is now replaced by consensus, where ferret journalism is played out, as people shop around for opinions that work for them, opinions they think will get the best play, the most attention, produce the biggest headlines. I have written a hard column at times. I take my shots, don't worry, at people like George Steinbrenner and anybody else I think deserves it. My column has run plenty of times under big back-page headlines. But people who think I have ripped my way into the jobs I have don't get it, and never will. I always came to this looking to celebrate sports.

It is just that sports keeps making it so goddamned hard.

Players shouldn't move around the way they do. Politicians shouldn't whore for owners the way they do. No kid should ever have to pay for an autograph. I'm not talking about the rules of sports here, I'm talking about the way things ought to be.

I am sick and tired of the unions running everything, sick of them sitting there smugly with their arms crossed and telling us we just don't understand every time we disagree with some new pit-bull thing they have done. I'm tired of ballplayers treating referees like garbage. You want a real Code of Conduct? Let some of these tough guys in sports pile up points on their records the way bad drivers do. Belle ended up getting a five-game suspension for his elbow to Vina's face (later changed to three games, and then two). Next time he steps out of line, in light of his rap sheet, make it ten games, or twenty, see if his manners improve then.

Let the guys on television start talking to the fans again, instead of the critics. Let them remember that their audience isn't limited to the powerful critics in New York, or Los Angeles, or in *USA Today*. The biggest guys in the industry constantly make fun of *USA Today*, and then grub around for mentions like dogs at the back door.

If they're actually quoted, you have to hose them down.

And let the owners of sports be what Robert Kraft of the Patriots says they're supposed to be. Let them really be caretakers of a public trust. Don't just listen to those people in the parking lot that Kraft talks about some of the time. Listen to them all the time. Listen to what they are saying, about the prices they pay, about the product, about some of these punks, about the way things are and the way they used to be.

One more time: Leave some money on the table.

Put games on when kids all over the country can see them, and if you take a hit at NBC or CBS or ABC or ESPN, well, that's part of it, that's a price you have to pay once in a while for the money that keeps blowing out of sports and through television like the tornado in *Twister*. Put a World Series game, at least one, in the afternoon. Not just one year, but every year. It's idiotic to have all these World Series games ending after midnight in the East. Same deal with games from the NBA finals ending just before midnight. And Monday Night Football.

In the writing of this book, I told my friend William Goldman one day about how I had cuffed around sports agents, and he read me something he had once written about agents in the movie business.

"Agents do not matter. They never have. They never will. Talent matters. Agents just live longer."

It is the same in sports. In the end, talent matters. A talent to hit a ball or throw a ball or dunk a ball, about which the rest of us can only dream. Sports is about the ones playing the game, and the ones watching. Not agents, not commissioners, not network suits, not union pit bulls, not the cheap hustlers from the sneaker companies, not the media.

Remember something: The song says "Take me out to the ballgame."

Not out to the cleaners.

And remember one other thing, always:

We've got them outnumbered.